Grazing the slopes of Matakana Valley

Publisher
Matakana School Board of Trustees

Creative Director
Peter Young

Book Design, Layout & Website
Lori Satterthwaite

Story Editor
Christine Sheehy

Food Editor
Emily Parker

Food Stylist
Kate Arbuthnot

Sponsorship
Laurette Macky

Food Photography
Lori Satterthwaite

Field Story Photography
Peter Young

Photo Shoot Coordinators
Amanda Garthwaite & Sally Jack

Editing, Proofreading & Indexing
Monique Thomas

Sub-editing & Proofreading
Anneliese Parker

Artwork
Katherine Norman

Lead Writers
Christine Sheehy & Helen Jamieson

Additional Photography
Katherine Norman

Additional Wild Food Festival Images
Louise M Photography

Additional Writers
Isaac Thackray, Kathy Hunter, Kaye Mueller, Carlie Blanchett-Burton, Rod Cheeseman

For more copies, visit www.thevillagetable.co.nz and follow us on Instagram @thevillagetable for updates.

Produced by Great Days Great Work LTD.

Printed in China.

ISBN: 978-0-473-44307-8

Title: The Village Table

Author: Various authors

Format: Hardcover

Publication Date: 10/2024

FSC
www.fsc.org
MIX
Paper | Supporting responsible forestry
FSC™ C007683

the VILLAGE TABLE

Recipes and stories from

MATAKANA

Contents

PAKIRI
WHANGARIPO VALLEY
LEIG
WHANGATEAU
Pt WELLS
OMA
BA
MATAKANA
SANDSPIT

Welcome

Welcome to The Village Table, a book inspired by our collective love of this land and the Matakana community.

Within these pages you'll find recipes and stories from some of the many artisans, producers and local heroes that give this place such heart.

Each chapter of this book celebrates a different 'village table' – places where we gather to enjoy food, friendship and the rich bounty of land and sea.

A true labour of love, it has been produced entirely by volunteers with recipes submitted by people in our community. All profits are going to Matakana School.

We are grateful for your support in purchasing the book and for all the businesses that have generously sponsored the chapters (please support them back).

We hope we have created something of the community, by the community and for the community.

Whether you're a local or a visitor, we look forward to seeing you at a village table sometime soon.

The Cookbook Team

The Matakana Village Farmers' Market has brought energy and creativity into our community every weekend for the past 14 years.

Long before you arrive at the bustling square, you'll hear the buzz of happy chatter, as artisans and producers trade their finely crafted wares for some hard earned cash. With a focus on fresh, sustainable and locally produced food, it is a Saturday morning must-do for locals and visitors alike.

Whether you come for the fresh produce, the delicious food, or to chill by the river enjoying live local music, this treasured weekly gathering offers a window on our region and the season.

Bring a basket and an empty belly – it's the perfect place to gather, enjoy a bite to eat and wind down into a Matakana weekend.

This chapter is brought to you by

Matakana Village
Farmers' Market

Breakfast

Matakana's Saturday morning must-do

PIPIS

Bag Lady

MATAKANA VILLAGE
CINEMAS
BARS
RESTAURANTS
SHOPPING

MEXI KANA
BURRITOS & NACHOS
MANDARIN MINT $5 GLASS
MENU

Perpetual
Silverbeet
Beetroot

THE MATAKANA

Angela Stechman & Lindesay Smith

LOVE IN EVERY CUP

It's Friday morning at Matakana Coffee Roasters. A local tradie tucks his muddy boots under the counter, cradling his long black and a breakfast burrito. A cast of regulars stop by after school drop-off and settle into the comfy armchairs. The tennis crew will be along soon, or the kids from the primary school, with a note requesting coffee for the staffroom.

'The Market is about local people selling things they've produced in a way that is honoured by labour and time'

Barista Christie Peacocke is the conductor of the scene and the ultimate keeper of nicknames and coffee preferences. She knows who's new in town and makes introductions accordingly.

For owners Angela Stechman and Lindesay Smith, who founded the Sierra chain of cafés prior to establishing Matakana Coffee Roasters, this is exactly how they like it. Coffee, they say, brings the community together. 'These people really matter to us,' says Angela.

Matakana Coffee Roasters was a founding stall when the Matakana Village Farmers' Market opened in 2004 and Lindesay has never tired of serving up coffee on a Saturday morning.

'The Market is about bringing together local people, to sell things they've produced in a way that is honoured by labour and time,' says Angela. 'We roast our coffee in small batches here in the village and put love in every cup.'

BREAKFAST BURRITO

The idea for the breakfast burrito came from one of Lindesay's long-standing customers at his former café in Herne Bay. It's quick to hand, nourishing and you can eat it on the run.

Angela Stechman & Lindesay Smith

SERVES: 1 | PREP: 5 MINS | COOK: 15 MINS | DIFFICULTY: BASIC

- **1 wrap**
- **HP sauce**
- **Handful of spinach**
- **1 rasher bacon**
- **4 pieces chorizo**
- **2 eggs**
- **1 tomato**
- **Herbs (sage, thyme, basil)**
- **Handful of mushrooms**
- **Dash of cream**
- **¼ cup cheese**
- **Aioli**

Drizzle HP sauce on the wrap. Place enough spinach on top of the sauce to cover the wrap.

Grill the bacon in the oven then cool, place one rasher of bacon on top of the spinach.

Grill your favourite chorizo in the oven and place 3-4 pieces on top of the bacon

Scramble the eggs, allow to cool, then place on top of the bacon.

Either bake tomatoes in the oven with a sprinkling of sage and thyme over the top or use freshly sliced tomato with a sprinkling of fresh basil. Place on top of the eggs.

Cook the mushrooms in a little bit of cream and allow to cool then add to the wrap.

Sprinkle with cheese and a drizzle of aioli. Fold the burrito up from the bottom, then fold each side over and use a bamboo skewer to keep it in place.

Heat on a panini grill until hot and the cheese has melted.

CHIA BERRY BREAKFAST

This is a yummy concoction of good things and can be served for breakfast, as an afternoon snack or as a dessert.

The Troope Family

SERVES: 2 | PREP: 20 MINS + CHILLING | COOK: 5-7 MINS | DIFFICULTY: BASIC

5 medium apples

3 bananas

1½ cups frozen berries

¼ cup chia seeds

1 cup sunflower seeds

1 cup pumpkin seeds

½ cup buckwheat groats

1½ cups rolled oats

Water

Peel and dice 4 apples and put into a pot to stew – you don't need to add any sugar, just cover the apples in water and heat until soft. Put aside until later.

Make a berry smoothie using 1 banana, 1 apple and 1 cup of frozen berries (choose your favourite or mix them up). Blend together with water in a NutriBullet or blender. After it has blended, stir ¼ cup of chia seeds into the smoothie and let it sit for 10 minutes.

Place the sunflower and pumpkin seeds in a blender and mix together to a rough consistency and stir in the buckwheat groats. This gives it a nice crunch. Put the seed mixture into the bottom of a bowl and press down firmly. Next layer the apple stew on top and take the remaining ½ cup of frozen berries and drop them into the apple stew, sharing between the bowls evenly.

Slice the banana evenly, layering on top of the apple and berries.

Then add about 2cm of rolled oats to completely cover the base and fruits and finish by layering the top with the berry chia smoothie.

Put into the fridge for 30 minutes or leave overnight so it's ready to eat straight away in the morning!

Notes: For a more nutritious twist, add spinach leaves or try sprouting your sunflower/pumpkin seeds and buckwheat groats before using them in the base.

You can also add nuts, spirulina or any other superfood to this mix.

BLACK STICKY BREAKFAST RICE

WITH MANGO

We love making this rice dish in our house as it's something we can put together ahead of time and change up depending on seasonal fruit. We chip away at it for days and have even been known to heat a little and serve with ice cream for an after dinner treat!

Sarah Willis

SERVES: 4 (SMALL) | PREP: 15 MINS | COOK: 50 MINS | DIFFICULTY: MEDIUM

1 cup glutinous black rice

3 cups water

2 cinnamon quills

1 piece orange rind

3 cups coconut milk

¼ cup coconut sugar

1 ripe mango

Juice from half a lemon

2 kaffir lime leaves

2 passionfruit

Coconut cream or coconut yoghurt

2 Tbsp flaked coconut, lightly toasted

Rinse rice then place into a pot with cold water, cinnamon quills and orange rind. Bring to the boil then reduce heat to a simmer for approximately 35 minutes, checking to make sure the rice doesn't completely dry up.

Add the coconut milk and sugar and continue to simmer until rice is tender and creamy, adding a little more milk if required.

Remove quills and rind, adding a little more sugar to taste. Allow to cool.

Remove flesh from the mango and blend in a food processor with the lemon juice and kaffir lime leaves until smooth. Add passionfruit pulp.

Assemble by layering rice with coconut cream or coconut yoghurt, then the fruit topping and lastly the toasted coconut.

BUCKWHEAT GRANOLA

Our family loves this homemade granola from Aaron Brunet because it tastes fresh and is so versatile. Make a large batch and keep it in an airtight container so it's ready anytime, or put some in a special jar wrapped with a ribbon and give it as a gift. We love it in winter with warm stewed fruit and in summer with fresh berries and yoghurt.

The Boyd-Wilson Family

SERVES: 500 GRAMS | PREP: 15 MINS | COOK: 1 HOUR | DIFFICULTY: EASY

3 ripe bananas
2 Tbsp honey
2 cups buckwheat
¾ cup sunflower seeds
1 cup dried coconut
2 tsp cinnamon
2 tsp dried ginger
½ tsp salt

Preheat oven to 150°C.

Mash the bananas in a bowl with honey. Add all remaining ingredients and mix well.

Spread onto a lined baking tray and bake for one hour until lightly browned.

Every 15 minutes gently mix around to avoid burnt edges.

Notes: Aim to retain clumps, only break them up if they're bigger than a small grape.

The granola may seem slightly damp when you take it out of the oven but it will dry as it cools.

If it is bone dry in the oven it will be extremely crunchy once cooled.

Add nuts or dried fruit once granola has cooled if desired.

Janis Grummitt

REWIRING THE BRAIN

When former workaholic Janis Grummitt began suffering from extreme exhaustion in 2007, no one suspected that a brain tumour the size of a large lemon had taken up residence in her frontal lobe.

After a gruelling treatment regimen including four brain surgeries, Janis discovered that the damage to her frontal lobe made her a more likely candidate for dementia. She became determined to rewire her brain.

'It slowly dawned on me that most people know more about their cell phones than they do about their brains,' says Janis. 'We notice our bodies deteriorating, but we think the brain will look after itself. From the age of 40, unless you do something about your brain, it will go downhill.'

Janis says that 'while physical, emotional and cognitive care are all vital factors in building an amazing brain, it all starts with the food we eat.'

'An amazing brain ... starts with the food we eat'

'What you eat and drink affects how much energy you have to exercise, which brings oxygen to the brain. It also affects the quality of your sleep, which is when the brain repairs and builds memories.'

'I try to get away from packets and eat whole foods as much as possible.'

Janis is on a mission to build a network of Wiring Warriors who can help spread the word about the importance of brain building. 'I would love to see Matakana have the lowest level of dementia in New Zealand.'

CHOCOLATE PORRIDGE

The addition of 70% dark chocolate transforms bland porridge into a decadent treat. Dark chocolate is full of antioxidants and as long as it's not full of sugar, it can be good for you too. Enjoy hot in winter and cold in summer.

Janis Grummitt

SERVES: 4-6 | PREP: 5 MINS + SOAK OVERNIGHT | COOK: 20 MINS | DIFFICULTY: BASIC

2 cups rolled oats

½ tsp salt

½ tsp cinnamon

½ tsp nutmeg

1 litre water

1 cup coconut cream

1 large, very ripe banana

5–6 pieces of dark chocolate (depending on your taste)

Mix the oats, salt and spices in a pot and cover with cold water and soak overnight.

Next morning, heat the oats until they boil, simmer, then add the coconut cream and cook for 20 minutes or until thick and creamy.

Remove from heat, stir in the 5 pieces of chocolate until melted, add mashed banana and mix thoroughly. Pour into a bowl for serving.

Notes: This is made without sugar, but if you prefer it sweeter, simply stir in some honey or maple syrup before serving.

To get the benefits of the chocolate, it must be dark, 70% cocoa or more and if possible, sugar free. The porridge can be made the day before and kept in the fridge then heated or served cold.

BUCKWHEAT BANANA PANCAKE STACK

WITH CHOCOLATE NUT BUTTER DRIZZLE

Buckwheat pancakes with banana have been a weekend treat in our household for donkey's years! These pancakes are sweet enough, so they don't need to be doused in maple syrup. This recipe will fill you up until lunch with a nourishing smile.

The Jackson Family

SERVES: 9 SMALL PANCAKES | PREP: 15 MINS | COOK: 10 MINS | DIFFICULTY: EASY

2 Tbsp ground flax seed or chia egg

6 Tbsp water

½ cup buckwheat flour

½ cup oat or coconut flour

1 tsp baking powder

½ tsp baking soda

¼ tsp sea salt

½ cup yoghurt (plain, soy or coconut) or thick coconut cream

¾ cup milk (nut or rice)

1 Tbsp maple syrup

1 tsp vanilla

1 tsp cinnamon

1 Tbsp melted coconut oil

2 bananas, sliced

Coconut oil for cooking

TOPPING:

½ cup blueberries, fresh or thawed from frozen

Generous drizzles of Almond and Chocolate from Matakana Nut Butters

To make the 'egg', soak the ground flax seed or chia in water for 15 minutes.

Preheat a large skillet over medium heat for 3-5 minutes while you make the batter.

Whisk together the flours, flax seed/chia egg, baking powder, baking soda and salt.

Add the yoghurt/coconut cream, milk, maple syrup, vanilla, cinnamon and coconut oil.

Mix until smooth, if you like thinner pancakes, add extra milk. Fold in sliced bananas.

Melt a teaspoon of coconut oil to grease the pan.

Let it heat for a minute, then add the batter a few tablespoons at a time.

The batter should sizzle when it hits the pan.

Cook for about 2 minutes on each side.

Serve warm, in a stack of 3, place blueberries on top, add additional fruit if desired, then simply drizzle the Almond and Chocolate nut butter straight from the jar over the top.

Notes: If you don't need the recipe to be vegan, add two eggs to the mixture instead of the chia or flax seed 'egg'.

Sophie & Michael Isbey

OCEAN TO TABLE

Sophie and Michael Isbey had been crewing on superyachts for six years, when they decided it was time to come home. They bought a 13.4-metre Jeanneau named Wanderlust (Lusty for short) in the Caribbean, sailing back via the Galapagos and the Pacific Islands. 'It was an amazing experience and a totally different pace of life,' says Sophie.

Both Sophie and Michael are keen on fishing, and a portable fish smoker installed at Lusty's stern ensured that no catch was ever wasted. Little did they know those smoking skills would soon take them into a new business.

'It's about giving world-class fish the TLC they deserve'

On arriving home, the couple found work selling beer for the Sawmill Brewery at the Matakana Village Farmers' Market and fell in love with the community. 'We knew we wanted to be part of it,' says Sophie. 'When the opportunity to buy Matakana Smokehouse came up, it was perfect.'

All Matakana Smokehouse products are 100% natural, sustainably farmed and fresh every week. Each piece of fish is smoked for at least seven hours with a blend of manuka, tawa, pohutukawa and other native botanicals 'It's about taking world class New Zealand salmon fillets, mackerel, kahawai, kingfish and sardines, and giving them the TLC they deserve.'

For these ocean-to-table foodies, this smoked fish kedgeree makes a satisfying breakfast on a lazy Sunday morning.

SMOKED MACKEREL KEDGEREE

Oily smoky fish, warm curry, turmeric and tart yoghurt come together to make this kedgeree a taste sensation. Make it with Matakana Smokehouse mackerel or kahawai. Top with poached eggs for the perfect weekend brunch.

Sophie & Michael Isbey

SERVES: 4 (SMALL) | PREP: 15 MINS | COOK: 50 MINS | DIFFICULTY: MEDIUM

6 cups water

1 Tbsp butter

2½ cups basmati rice

500g smoked fish (mackerel is great or kahawai or kingfish)

½ cup milk

1 cup cream

½ cup yoghurt

½ cup parsley, finely chopped

½ cup coriander, finely chopped

Salt and freshly ground black pepper

3 lemons

100g butter

2 large onions, finely diced

1 Tbsp garlic, minced

1 Tbsp ginger, minced

1 tsp mustard seeds

1 Tbsp (or to taste) fresh chilli, minced

1 Tbsp turmeric

½ Tbsp ground cumin

½ Tbsp garam masala

6 eggs (or however many people want, fried or poached)

In a large pot place 6 cups of water plus the tablespoon of butter and bring to the boil. Wash the rice under cold water, then stir into the boiling water. Reduce to a simmer, cover and cook for 20-25 minutes until all the water is absorbed and the rice is soft to bite. Fluff up the rice with a fork and set aside.

Place the flaked mackerel in a small pot. Add the milk and cream, place on a low heat and steep for 15 minutes just below simmering.

In a large pot place the butter, onions, garlic, ginger, mustard seeds and fresh chilli. Sauté over medium heat for a couple of minutes, then add the turmeric, cumin and garam masala. Reduce the heat to low and sweat for 20 minutes, stirring occasionally. Add the cooked rice and stir through to coat all the grains.

Now add the steeped mackerel to the rice and add the yoghurt. Stir to combine. Fold in the chopped parsley and coriander, then season with salt and pepper. Stir in the juice of one of the lemons and cut the other 2 into wedges. In another large pan, poach or fry eggs to your liking, runny yolks are particularly nice on top of the kedgeree.

Divide the kedgeree into warm bowls, place poached or fried eggs on top, garnish with a lemon wedge and coriander.

HOT MESS BREAKFAST BOWL

Healthy, warming and sustaining; this keeps us going for hours!

Melissa Coope

SERVES: 2 | PREP: 5 MINS | COOK: 5-7 MINS | DIFFICULTY: EASY

1-2 Tbsp oil (e.g. olive, coconut or avocado)

1 medium onion

Handful of mushrooms (e.g. button, portobello etc), roughly chopped

Additional vegetables if desired (e.g. zucchini, grated carrot, capsicum), chopped

2 large handfuls of green vegetables (e.g. kale with stalk removed, spinach, silverbeet, bok choy, beet greens etc), roughly chopped

Salt and pepper to taste

1-2 hot chillies, roughly chopped

2 eggs

Heat oil in frying pan.

Sauté onions, add mushrooms and other chopped vegetables next and greens last. Season with salt and pepper.

Add chilli if using.

Cook until vegetables are soft and greens are wilted (approximately 2-3 minutes).

Either crack eggs into the vegetable mixture and scramble, or move the vegetables into two "nests" and crack an egg into each nest.

If cracking an egg into a nest, flip each nest over when the egg white changes colour. If scrambling, stir through the vegetables until cooked.

Serve in a bowl with hot sauce of your choice on top (I love sriracha), sliced avocados when in season and a dollop of sauerkraut (homemade or bought, but raw for probiotic qualities and lovely sour flavour).

Get creative and top with other options such as sprouts, seeds and fresh herbs!

Notes: This is not a pretty meal but it is very tasty, especially on a cold winter morning!

For a child's palate omit the chilli and hot sauce when serving.

Richard & Christine Didsbury

BRINGING PEOPLE TOGETHER

In the early 2000s, as corner stores and local delis were regularly swallowed up by mega supermarkets, Richard and Christine Didsbury had a different vision for Matakana.

The couple purchased the old timber yard, with the idea of creating a destination village. There would be an arthouse cinema, boutique shops, communal spaces linking the main street to the almost-forgotten river's edge, and at the heart of it all, a farmers' market. 'Markets bring people together,' says Christine.

Back then most New Zealand markets were of the pop-up variety, selling a mixture of produce and bric-a-brac. When friends Trish Allen and Joe Polaischer of Rainbow Valley Farm shared photos of authentic farmers' markets they had visited in Japan, Christine became determined to do the same in Matakana.

'It's just lovely going to the market and seeing the enjoyment'

The focus would be firmly on locally grown food produced by the stallholders, with a certified commercial kitchen enabling them to meet compliance requirements.

The Matakana Village Farmers' Market opened in 2004 and was an instant success, drawing locals and visitors to enjoy food, music and community by the river's edge, all year round.

'The market has always been an incubator for small producers, and many have turned a home business into something much bigger,' says Christine. 'So many exciting things are unfolding, like the sustainable whitebait grown in Warkworth. The beer scene adds another element.

'It's just lovely going to the market and seeing the enjoyment people have.'

Matakana Village
Farmers' Market

Leigh Rd
MATAKANA VILLAGE
Medical Centre
Anglican Church
Art Gallery
SHOPPING
MATAKANA VILLAGE
TRAM
CAR
MATA
KANA

THE
MATAKANA

Matakana Village
Farmers' Market

TWIG + BLOOM
TEA & TONIC
MATAKANA
DÉ LOVELY
BOOKS
UPSTAIRS

Matthew & Gill Quested

POACHED TO PERFECTION

Throughout the 20 years she lived in London, Gill Quested had no inkling of a future life on the land.

But when her parents retired to the Mahurangi area, Gill and her husband Matthew, a born and bred Londoner, fell unexpectedly in love with the landscape. 'The rolling hills, the vastness of the countryside,' says Gill. 'We were hooked.'

The couple already had a few urban chickens and a keen interest in animal welfare. They could see that demand for free range eggs would grow in New Zealand, as it had in Europe.

'Establishing a commercially viable, free range chicken farm is extremely expensive,' says Gill. 'So we enrolled friends and family as investors in the business. Now, when they come from overseas to visit, they're just astounded by what they've helped create.'

'The rolling hills, the vastness of the countryside...we were hooked'

No wonder. Whangaripo Valley Eggs occupies 53 stunning hectares of rolling pasture and bush, criss-crossed by streams. Some 50,000 hens saunter about, scratching curiously in the grass, perching in the poplars and bathing in the dust. 'We're very proud of how well the chickens are looked after,' Gill smiles.

Now to the topic of the perfect poached egg – is there such a thing? 'Absolutely!' says Gill emphatically. 'The secret is in whether the egg is fresh.'

THE PERFECT POACHED EGG

The secret to perfect poaching is the freshness of the egg. If an egg is truly fresh, the white will hold its shape without the need to add vinegar or salt (which can cause the white to dissolve into the water).

Matthew & Gill Quested

SERVES: 4 | PREP: 5 MINS | COOK: 4-7 MINS | DIFFICULTY: EASY

4 fresh eggs

Fill a shallow frying pan with water. Bring to a gentle simmer - be sure not to boil.

Add up to a tablespoon of vinegar if desired, but if the eggs are fresh this is not necessary. Do not add salt - this may cause the egg white to break up.

Break the eggs into the barely simmering water. Poach for 3 minutes for a medium sized egg Lift out with a slotted spoon and drain on paper towels to avoid soggy toast. Season as desired.

Misty morning sunrise along Green Road, Matakana

Matakana Village
Farmers' Market

BAKED RICOTTA & CORNBREAD STACK

WITH TOMATO & ROCKET

Sunday mornings warming myself by the AGA, the smell of the cornbread and the baked tomatoes reminds me of autumn mornings in the UK.

Emily Parker

SERVES: 6–8 | PREP: 30 MINS | COOK: 1 HOUR | DIFFICULTY: EASY

375g polenta

375g self raising flour

Pinch of dry chilli flakes

2 cups buttermilk

1 cup extra virgin olive oil

4 eggs

100g parmesan cheese, grated

4 spring onions, finely chopped

250g corn kernels (fresh or frozen)

500g fresh ricotta

Extra virgin olive oil

Sea salt and pepper

2 ripe tomatoes

Handful of rocket per serve

Balsamic vinegar

Preheat oven to 160°C. Grease a loaf tin.

Mix all dry ingredients for the cornbread in a bowl, make a well in the centre.

Beat the wet ingredients together in another bowl and pour into the well.

Fold mixture together, add more buttermilk if it is too dry.

Pour mixture into the tin. Bake bread in the oven until it has risen and is golden brown.

Choose a small ovenproof dish for the ricotta. Pour in some olive oil and smear all over the bowl.

Place a generous pinch of salt and pepper on the base of the dish. Pack ricotta into the dish.

Drizzle some oil over the surface of the ricotta and more salt and pepper.

Place in the oven with the bread and bake until it has risen a little and is golden brown.

Remove and let cool.

Cook tomatoes in the oven at the same time, but they won't take as long.

Allow the bread and ricotta to cool until they are warm, cut both into slices.

Stack on a plate with bread, ricotta and tomato.

Place a few handfuls of rocket in a bowl and dress with oil, balsamic vinegar, salt and pepper.

Place the dressed leaves on top of your stack.

Matt Fox

MAKING GOOD BACON

Matt Fox was living in Holland with his partner Jasmijn de Graaf and their four children, when a series of European food scandals made him question food provenance. 'It made us really conscious about what's in the food we eat,' says Matt.

When the family relocated to Matakana in 2014, Matt became a regular shopper at the Matakana Village Farmers' Market, stocking up on fresh fish, veggies, cheese and bread. But one family favourite was missing – bacon.

Matt realised tasty processed meats are often packed with toxins, with little information about the meat's origins. So he did some research and discovered it was surprisingly easy to make honest bacon.

'I love seeing people try it for the first time'

'I asked Matt Watts at The Village Butchery to smoke some bacon,' he grins. 'He tasted it and said "We should be in business!"'

Thus the Matakana Bacon Company was born. A stall at the Farmers' Market quickly followed. 'I love seeing people try it for the first time. They're blown away by the taste – and then there's that look on their faces when they realise there's no rubbish in it.'

One such happy taster was marketing whizz Steve Charnley, who joined the business and is now expanding its reach through quality retailers. 'We're the only New Zealand bacon that is crate-free, sugar-free and nitrate-free,' says Matt. 'Other brands can only claim part of that list.'

BACON BUTTIES WITH AIOLI

My bacon buttie is a Sunday morning classic, made with fresh local ingredients. Who doesn't love bacon between two bits of bread with sauce? It's just win, win, win!

Matt Fox

SERVES: 1 | PREP: 10 MINS | COOK: 5 MINS | DIFFICULTY: BASIC

1 egg (free range), beaten

Salt and pepper

1 garlic clove, finely chopped

1 heaped Tbsp Dijon mustard

Generous pinch of curry powder

1 cup light olive oil (alternatively, use rice bran or grapeseed oil)

Apple cider vinegar

Chilli sauce or Sriracha (optional)

Start with a slice of double-baked sourdough from Plume Café, spread with a sweet relish from Puhoi Pantry or Black Earth kasundi if you like some pep.

Add biodynamic rocket from Kauri Creek Gardens and of course, Matakana Bacon - your choice of streaky or loin, grilled or pan fried to your liking.

Top it off with a drizzle of homemade aioli and another slice of sourdough.

Foxy's Easy Peasy Homemade Aioli:

Blend or beat the egg until creamy and season with salt, pepper, garlic, Dijon mustard and curry powder.

Blend again, slowly drizzling in the oil. Blend until thick and glossy.

Add a generous slosh of apple cider vinegar and a slosh of chilli sauce or Sriracha if desired.

Place the dressed leaves on top.

The aioli keeps well in an airtight container in the fridge.

THE VINTRY

ARTFORM
New Zealand formed by Hand.

Moni Jansen

THE TEA CONNOISSEUR

Simply stepping inside the peaceful environment that is Tea & Tonic in Matakana Village is enough to make you slow right down, and that's exactly what owner Moni Jansen intended.

Moni is a tea connoisseur and eager to share the benefits of taking time out of your day to let those leaves brew. 'Coffee can be quite rushed and functional – it's about getting that caffeine hit,' she smiles, 'but tea is a mindful drink.'

'Coffee can be quite rushed and functional ... but tea is a mindful drink'

With some reverence, Moni describes the intricacies of tea ceremonies she has attended. 'I've been to meditation tea ceremonies that go on for three hours, with a monk tea master pouring round after round.'

'Japanese tea ceremonies are all about attention to detail - how they place the cup, how they hold the teapot, how you hold the cup,' she continues. 'You never exhale on the tea as you would breathe out toxins. As you sip, you breathe in, which cools the tea.'

Moni is a wealth of knowledge on how teas can help with ailments. Her eyes light up as she describes how different varieties can boost health, relieve anxiety, balance hormones and even (by preparing and enjoying it) create social connection. 'And it looks so beautiful,' Moni says. 'Anything that's soothing for the mind and body can only be good.'

Beyond the teacup, Moni is also a committed advocate for sustainable business. 'At Tea & Tonic we're looking for organic ingredients, ethically made, with nothing harmful added – packaged in something home compostable, or else, glass.' ...Is it time for a cuppa yet?

Making the Perfect Cuppa

In selecting your tea, choose loose leaf, organic tea without added flavours. If you like fruit flavours try adding real raw ingredients to your teapot, like lemon or ginger slices, pomegranate seeds, apple slices, vanilla pod, peppermint leaves and berries.

Clay, porcelain or glass teapots and cups give the best flavour, as they do not react with the tea. Warm your pot and cups before making the tea.

1. 'Awaken' your tea leaves by pouring a little hot water onto the leaves, swirl briefly and then discard the water. This allows dust particles and any bitterness to be rinsed away and encourages the tea leaves to unfold.

2. Once you have boiled the water, leave it to stand 5 minutes before pouring over black tea, or 8-10 minutes for delicate white or green teas.

   Infusion times vary for each type of tea. Delicate green and white teas need only 30-60 seconds, while black tea requires 2-3 minutes of infusion time. Never leave the tea to 'stew' in the water. Instead, drain all the water off the leaves once the tea is ready and then you can reuse your leaves many times over.

3. Sit down and take a moment to fully enjoy the experience of your perfectly made cup of tea.

(With thanks to Catherine Opie, of BE Spa, supplier of artisan teas)

SPINACH & SAUSAGE FRITTATA

We are so lucky to be able to buy the terrific sausages that Greg Scopas of Salumeria Fontana makes to sell in Matakana. I love his range of sausages, but my favourite is the spicy sweet fennel sausages made from pure pork. The other essential ingredient is the bright yellow-yolked eggs I buy from Sandra of Waysand Farm.

Lauraine Jacobs

SERVES: 4 | PREP: 15 MINS | COOK: 15 MINS | DIFFICULTY: EASY

1 Tbsp extra virgin olive oil

8 Sicilian-style sweet fennel sausages (or other tasty sausages)

3-4 cups baby spinach leaves, washed

2 large onions

1 cup fresh herbs (thyme, basil, parsley), chopped

8 free range organic eggs

Salt and freshly ground black pepper

100g cheddar cheese, grated

Preheat oven to 175°C.

Fry the sausages in olive oil in a heavy frying pan until golden brown. Remove from the heat and when cool, cut each sausage into several slices. If there are more than 2-3 tablespoons of fat in the frying pan, tip some out.

Lower the heat, add the spinach and cook until wilted.

Remove from the pan and set aside to cool.

Slice the onions and add to the pan. Cook very slowly until the onions are soft, golden and nutty.

Spread the onions evenly across the base of the frying pan. Scatter half the herbs over the onions. Spread the sausages in a layer above this, then make a layer with the spinach.

Beat the eggs with the salt and freshly ground black pepper and pour over the vegetables.

Top with the remaining herbs and grated cheese and cook for about 2 minutes over a very low heat.

Remove the pan and place in the heated oven for about 3-4 minutes before switching to the grill option to nicely brown the top.

Serve warm or cold accompanied by spicy chutney.

Notes: I like to make this frittata in a frying pan that will go into the oven so that the top can be nicely browned under the grill.

This is also delicious served for lunch. Try it with a local Pinot Gris .

Juice
$7

Matakana Village
Farmers' Market
Please use our
DOG SITTING
SERVICE
Gold coin donation

TAMA

ROCKET
PARSLEY
$4
BASIL
$5
TOMMIES
$5

Matakana Village
Farmers' Market

Matakana Village Farmer's Market is a true foodie's heaven with a focus on fresh, sustainable and local artisan goods.

From award-winning coffee, to delicious brunch dishes, there's plenty to sample and savour. Relax by the riverside to live local music, while the kids explore the natural playground.

We're proud to say the Matakana Market is zero waste – so bring your baskets or bags and stock up on fresh produce, flowers, breads, deli treats and sweets.

2 Matakana Valley Road, Matakana
www.matakanavillage.co.nz/market/

Matakana Village
Farmers' Market
Saturday 8am - 1pm

Every Sunday morning over the summer, a group of hardy kids - and their parents - gather at Omaha beach for the Omaha Surf Lifesaving Club's 'young nippers' programme.

For the past 30 years the club has been a big part of our community, not only providing the volunteer lifeguards who patrol the beach, but ensuring there's a healthy supply of trainees coming up through the ranks as well.

With nearly four kilometres of white sandy beach, Omaha is a favoured spot for dog walkers, runners and surfers alike. The changing light, the luscious outlook to Ti Point and Hauturu Little Barrier, along with numerous playgrounds, tennis courts and walking and cycling trails, make Omaha an ideal spot to spend a day.

Our picnic recipes are packed with nourishing fare to satisfy even the most ravenous wannabe lifeguard. Spread a blanket and enjoy.

This chapter is brought to you by

BAYLEYS

Picnics

The 'little nippers' from Omaha Surf Life Saving Club

SURF LIFE SAVING

BAYLEYS

LAYERED COB LOAF

This loaf is an impressive and filling picnic dish. Making it the day before will enhance the flavours and you can vary the ingredients according to what you have on hand, or what is in season.

Hannah Hyslop

SERVES: 8 | PREP: 45-60 MINS | COOK: 10 MINS

Olive oil cooking spray

1 medium zucchini, thinly sliced lengthways

1 large eggplant, thinly sliced lengthways

300g orange sweet potato, peeled, thinly sliced into rounds

450g cob loaf

150g pesto

½ cup fresh basil leaves

200g roasted red capsicum

75g (6 slices) prosciutto

120g bocconcini, thinly sliced

½ cup semi-dried tomatoes, chopped

50g (8 slices) mild salami

Spray a large frying pan with oil. Heat over medium-high heat. Cook zucchini, eggplant and sweet potato in batches for 3-4 minutes each side or until browned and tender. Cool slightly.

Place loaf on a plate. Cut the top quarter from the loaf and reserve. Scoop out the centre, leaving a 2cm-thick shell. Spread pesto inside the loaf and the cut side of the top quarter.

Place sweet potato over the base of the loaf shell. Top with basil and then layer with capsicum, zucchini, prosciutto, bocconcini, tomatoes, eggplant and salami. Replace the top.

Wrap the loaf tightly in plastic wrap. Top with a plate and place a heavy object on top to compress the filling. Refrigerate overnight to develop flavours.

Preheat oven to 200°C. Unwrap loaf, place on a baking tray and bake for 5-7 minutes or until crust is crisp. Cut into wedges and serve.

Notes: You can substitute pesto with a chilli-based spread for more flavour.

CHICKEN LIVER & ORANGE PÂTÉ

This recipe is very special because it was created by my late sister who was an amazing cook. After she shared it with me, it became our signature pâté and friends and family would beg us to make it.

Joreen Smith

SERVES: 8-10 | PREP: 15 MINS | COOK: 30 MINS | DIFFICULTY: EASY

400g chicken livers, cleaned of any fat and rinsed in cold water

50g butter

1 onion, finely chopped

2 garlic cloves, chopped or crushed

3 rashers bacon or sliced ham, chopped

6-7 button mushrooms, diced small (optional)

75ml cream (optional)

100ml of alcohol of choice – Cointreau, brandy, sherry, port or a mixture of all

Ground black pepper

Fresh thyme or ½ tsp dried thyme

Parsley, chopped (optional)

Grated rind and juice of 1 orange

After rinsing the livers, place in a bowl, pour boiling water over and leave for 30 seconds.

Drain and chop coarsely in a food processor.

Sauté the onion and garlic in butter then add chopped livers. Cook while stirring occasionally for approximately 5 minutes.

Add bacon/ham, mushrooms, cream, alcohol, ground black pepper, herbs, orange rind and juice.

Cook for a further few minutes until everything is combined and reduced then either use a blender to make a very smooth pâté or a food processor for a slightly more textured terrine look.

Notes: Freezes beautifully in ramekins covered with two layers of cling wrap. Stir in a little more brandy or Cointreau before serving.

For a professional finish, gently heat 4 tablespoons of unsalted butter to clarify it, skim off the bubbles, lay a bay leaf on top then pour butter onto the pâté.

LAYERED SALAD

WITH CHILLI LIME DRESSING

Amazingly easy to make and such a fabulous idea for picnics, barbecues, travel snacks and lunch boxes. These layered salads keep fresh overnight and there is no need for any extra salad dressing as they're already dressed.

Nicole Ward

SERVES: 3 | PREP: 15 MINS | NO COOKING | DIFFICULTY: BASIC

¾ cup cooked brown rice

3 Tbsp cooked chickpeas

1 cup cherry tomatoes, sliced

½ cup feta cheese

2 Tbsp red onion, sliced

½ cup coriander, chopped

½ cup capsicum, diced

½ cup cucumber, sliced

½ cup iceberg lettuce, sliced

CHILLI LIME DRESSING:

4 Tbsp olive oil

3 Tbsp fresh lime juice

1 tsp dried ground cumin

Pinch of red pepper flakes

Salt and pepper to taste

Combine all dressing ingredients and then layer ingredients in a quart sized (1 litre) jar with a tight fitting lid in this order:

- chilli lime dressing
- cooked brown rice
- cooked chickpeas
- sliced cherry tomatoes
- feta cheese
- sliced red onions
- chopped coriander
- diced capsicum
- sliced cucumber
- sliced iceberg lettuce

When you're ready to serve the salad, close the lid and shake until emulsified.

Notes: Don't add ingredients to the jar that oxidise (go brown). For example, add avocado when serving.

If you want to make a salad half this size, use a pint sized jar (500ml) and halve the dressing ingredients.

Four kilometres of unbridled opportunity at Omaha beach

Josie Jackson

GOING FOR ZERO

When the Matakana Village Farmers' Market went zero waste at the end of 2016, Josie Jackson of Matakana Nut Butters was inspired to take a deeper look at her family's eco-friendly (and not-so-friendly) habits.

'We'd always been pretty good with recycling, reusable bags, chickens and compost, but I realised there was so much more we could do,' says Josie.

So she founded Zero Waste Matakana, a community network encouraging locals to reduce their waste. She's since organised workshops on making beeswax wraps (used in place of cling film), utensil kits for the car, homemade skincare products and waikawa, or woven flax food baskets. For plastic-free July, Josie held community sewing sessions to make fabric 'boomerang' bags for the village Four Square, as an alternative to plastic.

'I love teaching people because if they've gone to the effort of making it themselves, they're more likely to actually use it,' says Josie.

'It's not about being perfect – every bit counts'

She agrees that reducing waste takes a certain amount of organisation. 'Just like parents carry a baby bag, keep a zero waste kit in your car. Mine has reusable bags, a utensil kit, a 'keep cup' for coffee, cotton produce bags and glass containers for sushi or takeaways. It's not about being perfect – every bit counts.'

With major supermarket chains now committed to phasing out plastic bags, Josie's excited about the future of the zero waste movement. 'We have the power to drive change. Groups like ours in tiny communities all over the country are making big retailers pay attention.'

HOW TO HOST A ZERO WASTE PICNIC

- Stock up on some local deliciousness from the Matakana Village Farmers' Market. All the stallholders use compostable packaging or will be more than happy to fill your own container.
- Make your own thermos of tea or coffee and pack cups. Over 30 BILLION coffee cups end up in landfill each year.
- Bento lunch boxes, Tupperware containers and old jars are great ways to transport your picnic yummies, or use beeswax wraps to eliminate the need for plastic cling film.
- Pack utensil kits including cutlery and a straw. Plastic cutlery is a massive plastic polluter that we don't need.
- Fill your own water bottles, preferably glass, metal or BPA-free. Not only is water available from the kitchen tap, but you'll be doing your bit to reduce the billions of water bottles that enter landfill (only about 23% get recycled).

BEST BAKED OLIVES

Our eight-year-old is a huge olive lover, so we make these regularly. They are great to snack on and handy to have in the fridge.

Jo Meredith

SERVES: 3-4 | PREP: 5 MINS | COOK: 20 MINS

1 Tbsp chilli flakes

1 Tbsp fennel seeds

Zest of 1 lemon

4-6 garlic cloves, roughly chopped

⅓ cup olive oil

1 tin or jar black (or green) unpitted olives

Preheat oven to 150°C.

Place all ingredients except the olives in an ovenproof dish. The lemon can be zested or peeled off in thick slices with a vegetable peeler.

Drain the olives and cut the side of each with a sharp knife. Add to the other ingredients and mix so the olives are coated.

Bake in the oven for 20-25 minutes.

Notes: The excess olive oil is great as flavouring for other dishes or as a dip for breads.

BACON & EGG TOASTIE CUPS

This is a quick easy recipe where the ingredients can be individualised. I really love that they are single serves and made in a muffin tin so they can be cooked, cooled and packed straight in the chilly bin to take to the beach or park.

Angela Corinaldi

SERVES: 6 | PREP: 15 MINS | COOK: 15 MINS | DIFFICULTY: BASIC

2 slices bacon
½ spring onion
6 slices bread
6 eggs
¼ cup milk
Fresh thyme
Fresh parsley
Salt and pepper
6 cherry tomatoes, chopped

Preheat oven to 180°C.

Cook the bacon in a pan then cut into smaller pieces.

Cut the spring onion into small pieces.

Trim the crusts off the bread and butter one side.

Press the buttered side of each slice of bread into the cavity of a large muffin tin.

Lightly whisk the eggs in a separate bowl then add the milk, thyme, parsley, salt and pepper.

Add equal amounts of the cooked bacon, spring onion and tomatoes into each bread cup then add the egg mixture until each cup is three quarters full.

Bake for 15 minutes or until the egg is cooked.

Notes: You can change the ingredients based on what you have on hand such as mushrooms or capsicum for added flavour and vegetable content.

SCOTCH EGGS

When we go and visit our grandmother in England she always feeds us scotch eggs! They're yummy and good in your lunch box.

Ned & George Parker

SERVES: 8 | PREP: 40 MINS | COOK: 15 MINS | DIFFICULTY: MEDIUM

8 eggs, boiled for 4 mins (if you like them soft) or 8 mins (hard)

8 good quality sausages

½ tsp curry powder

1 tsp ground nutmeg

1 tsp hot English mustard

¼ cup herbs (parsley, chives, sage, thyme), chopped

1 tsp salt

Freshly ground pepper

Flour for dusting

2 eggs, lightly whisked and seasoned

2 cups breadcrumbs

Oil for cooking

Chutney to serve

Boil the eggs to your liking. Cool and peel carefully to keep them whole.

Split the sausages and squeeze all the meat out into a large bowl. Add the curry powder, nutmeg, mustard, chopped herbs, salt and pepper. Combine well using your hands. Divide the mixture into eight.

In the palm of your hand, flatten one of the balls of sausage meat. Place an egg in the middle, then encase it with the meat, carefully sealing the edges together. Damp hands help with this process. Continue with the remainder of the eggs.

Dust in flour, then dip in the egg and breadcrumbs to cover the whole ball. Place in the fridge for at least 30 minutes.

Fill a pot or deep fryer to ¾ full with flavourless oil. Bring it to 170°C, or when a bit of bread floats to the top it is ready. Place 2 or 3 scotch eggs in and cook for 5 minutes. If they brown too quickly the oil may be too hot.

The Scotch eggs may be eaten warm, or cool and refrigerate them until needed.

Serve with your favourite chutney or tomato sauce.

HEALTHY SEED CRACKERS

KNÄCKEBRÖD

This recipe was given to us by Poppa Pete. It's healthy and delicious and uses our family olive oil (Atutahi olive oil from Martinborough)

The Graham Family

SERVES: 8 | PREP: 10 MINS | COOK: 45 MINS | DIFFICULTY: EASY

100g cornmeal

30g sesame seeds

45g sunflower seeds

30g pumpkin seeds

40g linseed

60ml Atutahi extra virgin olive oil

½ tsp salt

250ml boiling water

Preheat oven to 150°C.

In a large bowl, combine cornmeal, sesame seeds, sunflower seeds, pumpkin seeds, linseed, olive oil and salt.

Slowly stir in the boiling water.

Using a spatula, spread the dough evenly over a sheet of baking paper, cover with a second sheet of baking paper and use a rolling pin to flatten the dough to about 3mm thick.

Use a pizza cutter disk to form rectangular pieces in the dough.

Bake for 45 minutes until golden and crisp. Allow to cool and then break into pieces.

Enjoy as a healthy snack on the go, or it also works very well as part of a cheese platter.

PESTO TORTE

The perfect 'bring-a-plate' or 'nibble' as it looks festive and colourful.

Sally Jack

SERVES: 10 | PREP: 20 MINS + CHILLING | NO COOK | DIFFICULTY: EASY

350g cream cheese, at room temperature

175g unsalted butter, melted

230g ricotta cheese, at room temperature

½ cup sun blush or sun dried tomatoes (cut if they are large)

½ cup pine nuts, lightly toasted

100g basil pesto

100g sun dried tomato pesto

Whip or process the cream cheese until smooth, add the melted butter and combine. Add ricotta and briefly combine. Divide the mixture into 3 parts for the 3 layers. Line a bowl with plastic wrap with excess wrap coming over the sides so you can cover later.

In the base of the bowl, place a circle of sun dried tomatoes and then a single layer of toasted pine nuts.

Spread the first layer of cream cheese mixture with a spatula then a thin layer of basil pesto and sprinkle with half the remaining pine nuts.

Spread a second layer of cream cheese mixture and cover this with a thin layer of sun-dried tomato pesto. Sprinkle the remaining pine nuts on top.

Spread the last layer of cream cheese mixture and cover with the excess plastic wrap. Chill for 3-4 hours or overnight. Place bowl upside down on a serving platter.

Serve with toasted Vogel's bread or plain crackers. You can also add basil leaves to the base of the bowl with the sun dried tomatoes.

Jenni Francis

CURATOR OF EVENTS

Want to know what's happening around town? Just ask local author, Jenni Francis.

Her weekly email newsletter, 'Around Matakana', is the quintessential guide to local events. Think intimate bluegrass jazz gigs at the Whangateau Hall, a night of storytelling at St Leonard's church in the village, composting workshops, book launches, film fundraisers and kombucha making classes – quirky cultural gems you'd easily miss if you didn't have a friend like Jenni 'in the know'.

Jenni moved to Matakana in 2003, just as the old timber yard was being transformed into the market square and village complex.

'Cooking is a way of connecting'

She joined the Matakana Community Group and as the area continued to grow, decided to start a newsletter to help spread the word about local businesses and events.

'There was so much happening and I wanted to get involved,' says Jenni.

When she's not broadcasting local happenings, you'll find Jenni singing in the Matakantata choir, working on her 'tweenage' novels, or trading her homegrown borlotti beans and blackberries at the Matakana Green Swap, where locals gather weekly or monthly (according to the season) to exchange excess produce.

'I never used to do this sort of thing when we lived in the city,' says Jenni. 'I've grown as a person since we came up here.'

The recipe for Lebanese open pies comes from Jenni's mother-in-law Hind, who arrived in New Zealand as a 19-year-old bride in 1950.

Almost seven decades on, the food legacy of Hind's childhood in Lebanon remains strong. 'Cooking is a way of connecting,' says Jenni. 'Hind still cooks a Lebanese meal for her sons every Sunday night.'

OPEN LEBANESE PIES

Like many Lebanese dishes, this recipe includes cinnamon to bring out the flavours of the minced lamb or goat. These pies are delicious hot or cold. I have included the full recipe, but if you're in a rush, just buy short pastry.

Jenni Francis

SERVES: 20 | PREP: 40 MINS | COOK: 20 MINS | DIFFICULTY: MEDIUM

FILLING:

500g minced lamb

2 onions

25g butter

150g cream cheese, softened

Juice of 2 lemons

½ tsp cinnamon

Salt and pepper

PASTRY:

25g butter

3 cups flour

½ tsp salt

1 tsp baking powder

Preheat oven to 180° C.

Brown the meat and onions in the butter, then cover with water and cook until the liquid has evaporated. Add the softened cream cheese, lemon juice, cinnamon, salt and pepper and mix well.

For the pastry, rub butter into dry ingredients, then mix in enough milk and water to make a scone-like dough. Roll this out very thinly (about ½cm or less) and using a 10-12cm cutter, make rounds from the dough.

Into the centre of each round, place a small teaspoon of meat mixture and pinch up the edges to make four corners, leaving the top open.

Place on a buttered tray and bake for about 20 minutes until golden.

Notes: Instead of making your own pastry, you can also use ready made short pastry. It took me years to figure out that's why my mother-in-law's pies always turned out so well!

CHICKEN, PUMPKIN & SUMAC FRITTERS

These are nutritious snacks that can be used for picnics, lunch boxes or eaten cold as a light lunch. The pumpkin gives them a sweetness that children will like.

Binty Bringans

SERVES: 4 | PREP: 20 MINS | COOK: 20 MINS | DIFFICULTY: EASY

1 cup self raising flour

2 eggs

¾ cup buttermilk

3 cups butternut pumpkin (squash), grated

1 cup mint leaves, chopped

1 Tbsp sumac, plus extra for sprinkling

2 spring onions, thinly sliced

2 cups cooked chicken, shredded

1 tsp sea salt flakes

Cracked black pepper

2 Tbsp extra virgin olive oil

Aioli to serve

Place the flour, eggs, buttermilk, pumpkin, mint, sumac, spring onions, chicken, salt and pepper in a large bowl and mix to combine.

Heat the oil in a large non-stick frying pan over medium heat.

Cook tablespoonfuls of the mixture in batches until golden brown and cooked through (about 6-7 minutes), turning once.

Add more oil with each batch.

Sprinkle with extra sumac and serve with aioli.

Notes: You can use poached chicken breast, leftover roast chicken or store bought roast chicken in this recipe.

Lauraine Jacobs

ROADSIDE BOUNTY

Since building her beach house at Omaha in 2003, Lauraine Jacobs has savoured the opportunity to eat locally grown, seasonal food.

'At the height of summer I can drive from Matakana to Omaha, stopping at ten farm stalls selling produce they've grown themselves,' says the well-known food writer and columnist for the NZ Listener.

'There are avocados, feijoas, grapes, apples, pumpkin and sweetcorn. There are flowers and watermelons, tomatoes and beans, and in winter, sweet mandarins. I don't think there's a potato in the country that tastes as good as those from Quail Farm.'

Back in 2008 Lauraine was so excited by the burgeoning local food scene that she literally wrote the book on *Matakana*, celebrating local food with recipes she created from the Village Farmers' Market.

'We're seeing spectacular developments in food, wine, art and beer'

Lauraine says the continually evolving food and wine scene is transforming the area into a desirable destination. 'Right now we're seeing spectacular developments in food, wine, art and beer. It's bringing people to the area and encouraging them to look below the surface.'

And while she loves escaping to Omaha, she says there's just one problem with life on the beachfront: 'You cannot grow anything, it's a pretty harsh environment'.

It is however, the perfect place to enjoy her salmon and spinach pie. 'My favourite picnic spot is right here on my front deck, with the remarkable view of Little and Great Barrier.'

Omaha Flats Road
NO EXIT

LOCAL
HONEY

Welcome to Quail Farm
Italian Courgettes $4.00
Capsicums $2
Limes $3
Chilli $2.00
Persimmons $4.50

DRIVE IN
PERSIMMON
MANDARINS
LIMES
CAPSICUMS
CHILLIES

TANGELOS

Ike's
MANDARINS
$5.00
per bag

BAYLEYS

SALMON & SPINACH PICNIC PIE

I have always thought that picnic food should be able to be eaten without the added nuisance of plates, forks and other paraphernalia. This pie is a real favourite of mine and nowhere near as heavy or rich as you might think. The secret is the wonderful flaky pastry and the light spinach and ricotta filling that complements the salmon.

Lauraine Jacobs

SERVES: 10 | PREP: 30 MINS | COOK: 30 MINS | DIFFICULTY: EASY

1 kg fresh salmon, skinned and boned

Salt and freshly ground black pepper

500g spinach

200g fresh ricotta cheese

Pinch of ground nutmeg

3 spring onions, chopped

2 Tbsp parsley or chervil, chopped

1 egg, beaten

500g flaky puff pastry

1 egg, beaten for glazing

Preheat oven to 200°C.

Season the salmon with salt and pepper and cut into 2 pieces down the middle lengthwise. Set aside.

Wash the spinach carefully to release any dirt and cook in a small amount of salted water until it wilts. Refresh under cold water and drain, squeezing out as much water as possible. Chop finely and add the ricotta, nutmeg, spring onions and herbs, mixing well and then add the beaten egg.

Roll out half the pastry to fit a medium rectangular pie dish with a loose base, making sure it hangs over the sides.

Spread half the spinach mixture into the tin on top of the pastry. Lay the salmon on top, topping and tailing the two pieces so that the shape of the salmon roughly fits the dish. Sprinkle over extra salt and pepper.

Carefully spread the remaining spinach mixture over the salmon.

Roll out the remaining pastry and place this on top, sealing to the pastry from the base by brushing with a little of the extra beaten egg.

Completely brush the pie with the remaining egg. Return to the refrigerator for at least half an hour to allow the pastry to rest so it doesn't shrink when baked.

Bake for about 30 minutes until the pastry is crisp and golden and the salmon is cooked. Perfect picnic fare served with spicy chutney.

Notes : If you can possibly find Paneton's frozen flaky puff pastry, please use it.

Serve with a good bottle of chilled Pinot Gris.

Hillside fun at Tawharanui Regional Park, Takatu Peninsula

The Greenwoods

GROWING TOGETHER

As the owner of Matakana Chillies, Tom Greenwood is familiar with the assumption that he likes hot food. 'People think you must be a chilli-head,' laughs Tom. 'It's just what I grow, though I eat a lot more now than I used to.'

Tom's great-great-grandfather was one of the first European settlers in the district. Tom grew up in the 140-year-old farmhouse that he now shares with his wife Sandra Bolland and their three daughters, Carlin, Tamsin and Esme.

'I enjoy growing and not being stuck inside'

'I enjoy growing and not being stuck inside,' says Tom. 'The beauty of chillies is that you don't have to pick them every day. That allows a lot of flexibility for the kids' sports and trips.'

Not to mention the community. For over a decade, Sandra and Tom have been involved in many local voluntary activities. From co-ordinating junior surf life saving, to coaching hockey and acting as club secretary, organising the mammoth 'sorting' of donations for the school gala, setting up the school marquee at sports events or whipping up meals for those in need. If there's a job to be done, Sandra and Tom are the first to lend a hand.

'Sandra will always say "yes" when she's asked to help and she gives it 100 per cent,' says Tom. 'If it gets too big, she'll convince me to help too!'

Sandra's stuffed jalapeños are a favourite for picnics and bring-a-plate occasions - a little spicy, a little sweet, and easy to whip up at short notice.

JALAPEÑOS WITH CREAM CHEESE

We love sharing these chillies with friends for picnics and pre-dinner nibbles. They can be eaten hot or cold and pair well with an icy cold Corona.

The Greenwood Family

SERVES: 10-12 | PREP: 10 MINS | COOK: 20-25 MINS | DIFFICULTY: EASY

10 fresh green jalapeño chillies

225g cream cheese

Smoked paprika to sprinkle on top

Preheat oven to 180°C.

Cut the chillies in half lengthwise and scrape out the seeds with a knife or teaspoon (or keep the seeds in if you like them hot).

Using a knife, spread cream cheese in the jalapeño halves.

Place on an oven try or in a roasting dish, cream cheese side up.

Sprinkle with smoked paprika.

Bake for 20-25 minutes.

ANN'S ROCKY ROAD

This was my sister's recipe, a definite comfort food. It is very special to our family as it reminds us of her. She passed away 5 years ago from cancer.

The Hames Family

SERVES: 20 | PREP: 5-10 MINS + CHILLING | COOK: 10 MINS | DIFFICULTY: EASY

1-2 packets MallowPuffs

1 packet marshmallows

¾ cup brown sugar

200g butter

1 egg, beaten

1 large size block chocolate

Line a 23cm round cake tin or a 20cm square tin with baking paper.

Cut off the base of the MallowPuff biscuits and line the tin with these, chocolate side down. Chop up the MallowPuff tops and marshmallows and fill in any spaces between the biscuits. Also layer the marshmallows over the biscuits.

In a pot, bring brown sugar, butter and beaten egg to the boil. Boil for approximately 3 minutes, stirring continuously so it doesn't burn. It will turn into a thickened caramel mixture. Allow to cool and whisk occasionally for a smooth consistency. Pour over the base and refrigerate.

Melt the chocolate using a double boiler, pour over the base and return to the fridge to set. Once firm, cut into bite sized pieces.

ENERGY BALLS

These energy balls are an all-time favourite for our children, Taylor and Maeve. A delicious blend of dates and nuts and raw cacao make for a seriously yummy, filling and healthy snack! They're also super easy!

The Davids Family

SERVES: 10-12 | PREP: 10 MINS + SOAK OVERNIGHT | NO COOKING | DIFFICULTY: EASY

1 cup almonds or pecans, soaked overnight

1 cup dates, soaked overnight

½ tsp vanilla essence or 1-2 vanilla pods

2-3 Tbsp raw cacao powder

1 Tbsp desiccated coconut (optional)

1 Tbsp chia seeds (optional)

Place the soaked, drained nuts into a food processor. Blend until they resemble a rice-like consistency.

Add the soaked, drained dates into the food processor. Add the vanilla or open up a vanilla pod, scrape out the middle and add to the mix. Add the cacao powder. Blend until it forms a sticky consistency.

Use a tablespoon to scoop out small amounts of the mixture into clean hands and roll into balls between your palms. Roll the finished energy balls in the desiccated coconut for a 'sprinkled' and delicious effect.

Place in a container and refrigerate for at least 2 hours. Keep in the fridge for freshness. Yum!

Notes: Add the chia seeds to the mixture for added energy.

Go camping or have a picnic and surf at Tawharanui Regional Park

CHEESECAKE IN A JAR

The tui are singing, the piwakawaka are dancing. It's summer and your friends and whanau will sing and dance too when you arrive at a picnic with this stylish dessert. A creamy blueberry cheesecake in a jar? Stop it! It's a real crowd pleaser. Did somebody say cheesecake?

Charlie & Barnaby Blampied

SERVES: 6 | PREP: 30 MINS | COOK: 2 MINS | DIFFICULTY: BASIC

14 whole digestive biscuits (the gluten-free variety work great too)

4 Tbsp unsalted butter, melted

2½ cups fresh blueberries (you can use any fresh or frozen fruit)

Juice of ½ lemon

1 Tbsp caster sugar

450g cream cheese

1 tsp vanilla extract

½ cup icing sugar

¾ cup heavy cream

Lemon zest

Put digestive biscuits into a large bowl and crush into crumbs using the end of a rolling pin. Mix in the melted butter until thoroughly combined. Put to one side.

Place the blueberries, lemon juice and caster sugar in a pan and heat gently until the blueberries start to break down and the liquid is hot and the blueberry mixture has thickened. Turn off the heat and allow to cool.

Place the cream cheese in a bowl and mix with a hand whisk until the cream cheese has become smooth in consistency. Add the vanilla extract and icing sugar, then whisk again until combined.

Whisk the cream in a separate bowl until thick, but still soft.

Spoon the whipped cream into the cream cheese and gently stir to combine.

Spoon 3 heaped tablespoons of the biscuit crumbs into the bottom of a mason jar and push down with a spoon or the end of a small rolling pin. Gently spoon on 2 heaped tablespoons of the cream cheese mixture and level it. Add 2 tablespoons of the blueberry mixture.

Repeat for the other jars, then top with a little lemon zest. Put the lid on and refrigerate until needed.

Notes: The beauty of this recipe is that you can make it gluten free if you wish, by using gluten free oat crackers or biscuits instead of digestive biscuits. You can also reduce the sugar content or make it with honey to be more natural. Create variety by using seasonal fruit and serve it in winter after dinner while the sauce is still warm on the stove. They can be served in pretty little jars for an extra wow factor.

Sitting down for a picnic at Omaha

CHICKEN TERRINE

WITH PRUNES, APRICOTS & PISTACHIOS

Deliciously simple and flavoursome, this terrine is ideal to take on a picnic.

The Team at Bayleys

SERVES: 8 | PREP: 20 MINS | COOK: 1½ HOURS | DIFFICULTY: EASY

250g sliced streaky bacon

20g butter

1 onion, diced

250g chicken breast

500g chicken mince

100g dried apricots, chopped

50g prunes, chopped

50g pistachio nuts, chopped

1 tsp salt

1 tsp freshly ground black pepper

50g bacon, chopped

Preheat oven to 160°C.

Line a loaf tin with streaky bacon.

Melt the butter and sauté the onion until translucent.

Remove skin from chicken breasts and reserve. Chop the chicken into large chunks.

In a large bowl thoroughly mix all ingredients except the chicken skin and chopped bacon. Pack into the lined tin and cover with the chopped bacon followed by the reserved chicken skin (the chicken skin prevents burning).

Bake for 1½ hours. Remove from the oven and allow to cool. Drain off the excess liquid and remove and discard the chicken skin. Remove from the tin, wrap in foil and refrigerate overnight.

Serve sliced with pickles and salad. If you wish, drizzle with a little olive oil.

Notes: Will keep in the fridge for 4-5 days.

SOLD

Our team are as passionate about Matakana and the broader local area as we are about getting great results for our clients.
We practise what we preach and are proud supporters of our community, from Matakana School to the local rugby, hockey, cricket and golf clubs, the Warkworth A&P Show and many more community groups.
We offer a strong and dedicated team of local professionals. With local offices in Matakana, Omaha and Warkworth we've got the market covered and with our marketing reach we can find buyers that others can't.
If you're looking for quality advice in a down-to-earth and friendly manner, the team at Bayleys would love to be able to help.
09 425 7640
www.bayleys.co.nz
LICENCED UNDER REA
BAYLEYS
Sale
HOME

NEW WORLD
Sausages Greek
16 99
15 99
15 59
13 99
20 99
3 99

BAKELS
NEW ZEALAND
SUPREME PIE
Beef, Blue Cheese & Mustard Pie
6.49
ea
Product of New Zealand

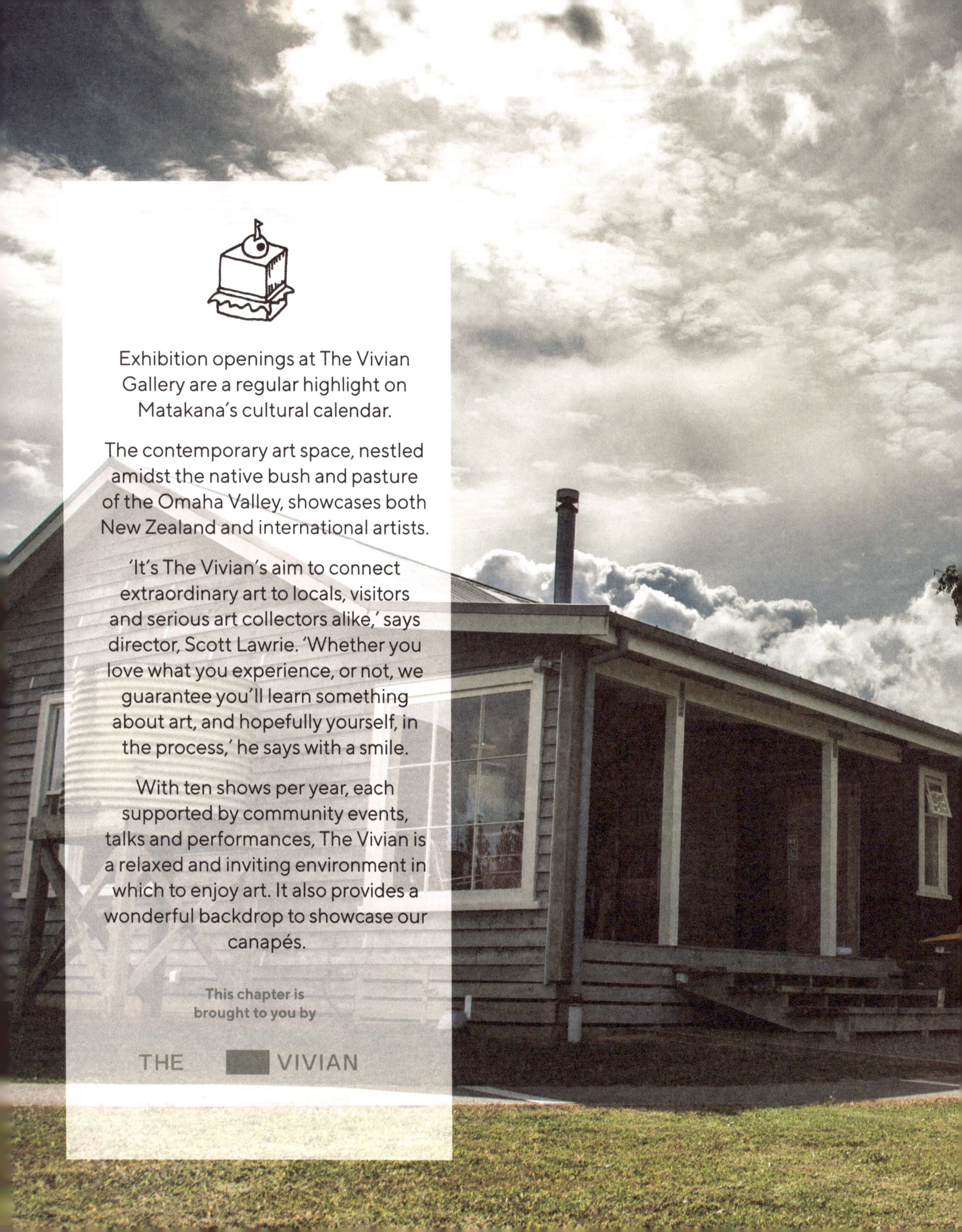

Exhibition openings at The Vivian Gallery are a regular highlight on Matakana's cultural calendar.

The contemporary art space, nestled amidst the native bush and pasture of the Omaha Valley, showcases both New Zealand and international artists.

'It's The Vivian's aim to connect extraordinary art to locals, visitors and serious art collectors alike,' says director, Scott Lawrie. 'Whether you love what you experience, or not, we guarantee you'll learn something about art, and hopefully yourself, in the process,' he says with a smile.

With ten shows per year, each supported by community events, talks and performances, The Vivian is a relaxed and inviting environment in which to enjoy art. It also provides a wonderful backdrop to showcase our canapés.

This chapter is brought to you by

THE VIVIAN

Canapés

The Vivian Gallery, Omaha Valley

Scott Lawrie

Omaha Valley Rd No Exit
The Vivian Gallery

MINI CARAMELISED ONION & FETA TARTS

WITH HONEY DRIZZLE

These mini tarts are a yummy combination of sweet, creamy and tangy and they're also super quick to prepare. They're perfect for parties, picnics or even just a snack.

Tracy Blair

SERVES: 24 | PREP: 30 MINS + CHILLING | COOK: 1 HOUR | DIFFICULTY: EASY

PASTRY:

180g butter, chilled

2 egg yolks

Pinch of salt

225g plain flour

FILLING:

6 onions, thinly sliced

1 cup water

1 tsp sea salt

3 Tbsp balsamic vinegar

2 Tbsp brown sugar

1 egg yolk, beaten with a dash of milk

150g feta cheese, crumbled

Freshly ground pepper

2 tsp thyme

Honey for drizzling

To make the pastry, put the butter, egg yolks and salt in a food processor and blitz. Blend in the flour and work into a dough. Chill for at least 1 hour.

For the filling, combine the onions, water, sea salt, balsamic vinegar and brown sugar in a large pot. Cover and cook on medium for 15 minutes. Remove the lid, reduce heat and cook, stirring occasionally, for another 15-20 minutes until the liquid has all but evaporated and the onions are very soft. Allow to cool.

Preheat oven to 160°C. Prepare your non-stick or greased mini tart pans.

Remove the dough from the fridge. Using a rolling pin, roll it out on a floured surface, lifting and turning the pastry occasionally.

Use a cutter to punch discs from the rolled pastry for your individual tart cases. Use your fingers to work in each pastry disc. Pleat the edges of the dough circle, thereby creating a pocket that sinks into the tartlet case. Shape gently inward and trim edges neatly by pinching off excess with your fingers. Brush the border of the pastry with the egg yolk/milk mixture.

Fill your tart cases with baking beans and blind bake for about 10-15 minutes, or until just turning brown. Take out of the oven and cool.

Spoon the caramelised onion mixture into the pastry shells. Crumble the feta over the top, add some black pepper and sprinkle over the thyme.

Place back into the oven for a further 10-15 minutes until golden and crisp. Drizzle with honey.

Notes: The pastry shells can be made ahead and frozen or you can buy ready made pastry. The onion mix can also be made ahead.

SMOKED SALMON DILL CRÈME & CUCUMBER

These canapés are small enough to eat in one bite, and light and tasty enough that you can enjoy them without ruining your main course (and dessert)!

Anneliese Parker

SERVES: 20 | PREP: 15 MINS + CHILLING | NO COOK | DIFFICULTY: BASIC

- **¾ cup sour cream or crème fraiche**
- **1½ Tbsp fresh dill, chopped (or use 1 tsp dill paste)**
- **Zest of ½ lemon, finely grated**
- **1-2 Tbsp lemon juice**
- **150-200g hot smoked salmon**
- **Salt and freshly ground black pepper**
- **2 Lebanese cucumbers**
- **Extra sprigs of dill**

In a bowl mix sour cream/crème fraiche, dill, lemon zest and lemon juice until smooth.

Flake salmon flesh (discard skin) into the bowl and gently fold to combine.

Season to taste with salt and freshly ground black pepper.

Place in the fridge for at least 30 minutes to firm up a little, until ready to serve.

Wash and slice cucumbers into 5mm thick rounds – you should get 20 rounds.

To assemble, spoon a teaspoon of salmon and dill crème onto each cucumber slice. Garnish with a little fresh dill.

Serve within 30 minutes.

Notes: You can replace the dill with fresh fennel frond for a flavour change.

WATERMELON & HALLOUMI NIBBLES

Our family love watermelon so much we sowed a huge patch in our paddock. Once the first 300 hundred balls of juicy red deliciousness were big enough to pick, we loved sharing them with friends. Throw some halloumi on the BBQ and add fresh mint from the garden for a fresh, sweet, hot and salty taste of summer. Best served with an afternoon G&T.

Chelsea De Berry

SERVES: 20 | PREP: 20 MINS | COOK: 2 MINS | DIFFICULTY: BASIC

1 watermelon (or half depending on how many you are feeding)

1 packet halloumi cheese

Coconut oil for cooking

Lemon

Chilli flakes

Fresh mint leaves, chopped

Himalayan pink salt

Cracked pepper

Cut watermelon into 5 x 5 x 3cm squares and place on a platter.

Cut halloumi into strips and then squares. Heat coconut oil in a pan and quickly brown the cheese (don't cook for too long as it will go gooey).

Place a piece of halloumi on each piece of watermelon.

Squeeze ½ lemon all over and then sprinkle over chilli flakes and a handful of chopped mint leaves. Add Himalayan pink salt and cracked pepper.

The annual athletics day

Dan O'Donnell

ASIAN FARE WITH A TWIST

From his classical French training, to his days as head chef at Prego in Ponsonby and his own successful bistro-style restaurants, Dan O'Donnell has some serious culinary pedigree.

In 2015 Dan decided that he - and by extension Matakana - needed a little more spice. So he set off on a gastronomic tour of South East Asia, soaking up the fresh flavours and high energy cooking in markets and restaurants across Thailand, Vietnam and Singapore, before launching his latest restaurant venture.

'The hardest thing was finding someone who could make the buns properly'

Jin Jin serves up authentic Asian fare with a twist. Dan prides himself on making everything from scratch, with real ingredients, and refuses to load his dishes with sugar just to make them acceptable to Kiwi palates.

One of Jin Jin's most popular dishes is the simple yet deceptively delicious Pork Bun. But the journey from Dan's mind to the table was not without its challenges.

'The hardest thing was finding someone who could make the buns properly,' says Dan. 'We sell hundreds every week.' That search took him to a specialist Chinese baker in South Auckland, who bakes the buns to perfection every time.

But a pork bun can only achieve true greatness when accompanied by an exceptionally delicious hoisin sauce. Dan's house-made version is a time-consuming recipe, but he says the home cook can achieve a great result by jazzing up a bottle of Lee Kum Kee Hoisin Sauce from the supermarket. 'Add some orange zest and a squeeze of lime juice,' says Dan. 'It makes the sauce less sticky and cuts through the salt and fat of the pork.'

PORK BUN

This recipe is a make-at-home version of one of Jin Jin's most popular dishes, loved by adults and kids alike.

Dan O'Donnell

SERVES: 18 | PREP: 2 DAYS | COOK: 3½ HOURS | DIFFICULTY: MEDIUM

BUN DOUGH:

175ml warm water

10g dried yeast

1 Tbsp sugar

2 Tbsp oil (rice bran)

375g plain flour

ROAST PORK:

2kg pork belly

100g Chinese Five Spice

100g coarse ground black pepper

600g salt, divided

PICKLED CUCUMBER:

1 cucumber

1 tsp sugar

1 Tbsp lime juice

Chilli or chilli oil

Salt and pepper

SAUCE:

Lee Kum Kee Hoisin sauce

Orange zest

Squeeze of lime

Coriander

For the bun, combine water and yeast, leave for a few minutes to activate. Once foamy, add the sugar and oil and mix with flour in a large bowl (use a food processor if you prefer) until it's super smooth. This may take 15 minutes.

Roll the dough into a large sausage shape about 5cm in diameter and cut into approximately 18 slices. Roll each one into a rounded rectangle and place on baking paper cut into hand-sized pieces. Place on a tray and cover with a damp tea towel or paper towels and leave in a warm place to rise. Once doubled in size they are ready for steaming.

For the steaming, a traditional Chinese steamer is preferable, otherwise you can create steam using a pot with a lid. Raise a rack to about the water level, put on a lid and you have a steamer. Once you have steam, cook the dough for 20 minutes, take out and fold in half and allow to rest.

To prepare the pork belly, place skin side down on a rack (on top of a roasting tray) so the meaty side is exposed. Mix the five spice, pepper and 100g of salt together and rub into the meat. Allow it to sit for 10 minutes.

Flip over so the skin (soon to be crackling) is facing up, cover with 500g salt then cover with a tea towel or paper towels and place in the fridge overnight. The next day, clean all the salt off the pork and dry.

Preheat the oven to 200°C on fan grill or fan bake if you can isolate the top element.

Put water in a roasting tray, about 2.5cm deep and put the pork on top of the rack, place in the oven and cook until the skin has turned golden and has crackled (approximately 1 hour). Turn the oven down to 150°C and cook on bake for another 2 hours then remove from oven, take the rack off the tray and leave to cool.

To make the pickled cucumber, remove half of the cucumber skin with a peeler, cut into desired size rounds and place in a bowl. Add the sugar, lime juice, chilli (or chilli oil) and a sprinkle of salt and pepper. Place in the fridge to chill.

To assemble, get your steamed buns, add sliced roast pork, pickled cucumber, hoisin sauce (add some orange zest and a squeeze of lime to the hoisin) and coriander. Enjoy!

The view across Sugarloaf to Mt Tamahunga

BAKED ARTICHOKE DIP

A delicious dip that's yummy served hot or cold. If there is any left over, it's also great spread onto a crusty slice of bread, grilled as a toastie and served with a bowl of soup. Enjoy!

The MacFarlane Family

SERVES: 10 | PREP: 10 MINS | COOK: 35 MINS | DIFFICULTY: EASY

3 Tbsp olive oil

2 onions, sliced

2 garlic cloves, crushed

2 Tbsp fresh thyme leaves

Salt

400g tin cooked artichokes, drained

100g cream cheese, at room temperature

½ cup parmesan cheese, grated

⅔ cup sour cream

Zest of 1 lemon

1 egg

Salt and pepper

TOPPING:

3 Tbsp cream

3 Tbsp parmesan cheese, grated

Preheat oven to 180°C.

Heat oil in a sauté pan, add the onions, garlic, thyme and a pinch of salt.

Cover and cook for 10 minutes.

Uncover and cook onions until tender and slightly caramelised.

Transfer to a bowl and cool.

Quarter the artichokes and place them between a paper towel to remove the liquid.

Blend cream cheese, parmesan, sour cream, lemon zest and egg in a food processor until smooth. Add the artichokes and pulse until chunky.

Tip into the bowl with the cooled onions, season and stir.

Place mixture in a gratin dish, spoon over the cream and sprinkle on the parmesan.

Bake for 25 minutes until set and golden.

Serve warm or at room temperature.

ROSSIE'S CHEESE ROLL

This recipe has been handed down through the generations and it's delicious served as a pre-dinner nibble or after dinner on a cheese board with your favourite crackers.

Matt Vyle

SERVES: 12 | PREP: 20 MINS | NO COOKING | DIFFICULTY: EASY

50g cream cheese

170g blue vein cheese

1 garlic clove, crushed

½ tsp dry mustard

2 tsp Worcestershire sauce

60g butter

½ cup brown sugar

½ tsp dry mustard

¼ tsp curry powder

1½ cups pecans, finely chopped

Mix cream cheese, blue vein cheese, garlic, mustard and Worcestershire sauce together in a bowl and make into two logs approximately 20cm long and place on foil.

Roll them up and refrigerate while you prepare the topping.

For the topping, melt the butter and add the remaining ingredients.

Mix well and spread the topping over the log.

Serve immediately or wrap again in foil and refrigerate.

Notes: This is excellent served before dinner or after dinner with a platter including grapes and dessert dates.

MOZZARELLA & RISOTTO BALLS

These little balls are really easy to make but will impress your guests. It's a great way to use up leftover risotto. They are a huge hit with adults and kids alike (you can even sneak a few hidden vegetables in).

Pene Fox

SERVES: 6 | PREP: 20 MINS | COOK: 5 MINS | DIFFICULTY: BASIC

2 cups (approx) prepared leftover risotto, cooled

100g smoked mozzarella, cut into 1cm cubes

½ cup flour

Salt and pepper

2 cups breadcrumbs

3 eggs, lightly whisked

750ml canola oil

Aioli

Take a small tablespoon of cold risotto and fill it with a cube of mozzarella.

Shape the risotto to cover the cheese and roll it into a neat ball. Continue until all the risotto is used. In a shallow bowl, mix the flour with some salt and pepper.

Place the breadcrumbs in another shallow bowl and the eggs in another.

Dip each risotto ball into the seasoned flour, then the egg and lastly the breadcrumbs, covering it all over.

Place on a clean plate and repeat. Heat the oil to about 180°C, then fry the risotto balls in batches until golden all over – about 3 minutes. Serve with aioli.

Notes: any flavour risotto will do, but I usually flavour mine with saffron.

BITTERBALLEN

Bitterballen are a satisfying Dutch beer snack, served in almost every bar and restaurant in the Netherlands. Similar to a beef croquette, the crunchy exterior gives way to delicious beef and gravy.

Will Michell

SERVES: 20 BALLS | PREP: 30 MINS + CHILL OVERNIGHT | COOK: 20 MINS + 3-4 HOURS BRAISING | DIFFICULTY: EASY

1 onion
2 tomatoes
750g – 1kg beef brisket to yield 500g shredded beef
500ml red wine
1 litre beef stock
1 brown onion
250g butter
250g plain flour
650ml beef stock
350ml braising stock
Plain flour, extra
2 eggs, whisked
Breadcrumbs
Vegetable oil for frying
Mustard and aioli to serve

Preheat oven to 180°C.

To slowly braise the beef brisket, roughly chop 1 onion and 2 tomatoes and place in an oven tray. Lay the beef brisket on top of the vegetables and cover with red wine and 1 litre of beef stock.

Cover with foil and cook for approximately 3-4 hours until the meat is falling apart. Remove from the oven, discard the onion, shred the meat and reserve the braising stock.

In a large wide based pot, fry the onion in butter until the butter starts to brown. Add flour and stir using a wooden spoon, cooking until the flour mixture starts to smell biscuity.

Pour in 650ml of beef stock and 350ml of reserved braising stock and whisk. The mixture should soak up all of the stock. Remove from heat and add the shredded beef, mixing thoroughly. Pour the mixture into a tray, cover and refrigerate overnight.

Roll a heaped tablespoon of mixture into a ball, roll in flour, dip in egg and then crumb. Repeat with the remaining mixture.

Heat oil to 180°C and fry until golden brown.

Serve hot with aioli and a grainy or hot mustard.

LEMONGRASS PRAWN SKEWERS

Time poor, bereft of cooking skills and fearful when someone asks you to 'bring a plate'? Then this wee gem is the one for you! We discovered this while living in Hong Kong and it's delicious.

The Forsyth Family

SERVES: 4 | PREP: 30 MINS | COOK: 10 MINS | DIFFICULTY: EASY

600g raw king prawns, shelled, deveined, diced

1 Tbsp fish sauce

1 garlic clove, finely chopped

1 red chilli, deseeded, finely chopped

1 spring onion, finely sliced

1 Tbsp iced water

5 Tbsp sesame seeds

3 long thin lemongrass stalks, cut into 8cm sticks (you'll need 12 sticks)

⅓ cup coconut oil, melted

Salt and pepper

1 lime, halved

LIME DIPPING SAUCE:

1 small red chilli, roughly chopped

1 garlic clove, chopped

2 Tbsp fish sauce

2 limes, juiced

3 Tbsp water

To make the lime dipping sauce, pound the chilli and garlic using a mortar and pestle until almost smooth. Stir in the fish sauce, lime juice and water. Add more fish or lime juice if needed. Set aside.

Process the prawns in a food processor until smooth and sticky. Add fish sauce, garlic, chilli and spring onion and pulse to combine. Add water to form a thick, coarse paste.

Wipe your hands with oil or water, then divide the prawn mixture into 12 portions and roll them into sausage shapes.

Place sesame seeds in a small bowl and roll the prawn sausages in the seeds to coat.

Thread the prawn mixture onto the lemongrass sticks and roll them in the sesame seeds again.

Brush with a little oil.

Preheat BBQ or frying pan and brush with coconut oil.

Cook prawn skewers for 5 minutes, turning occasionally, until golden brown and cooked through. Sprinkle with salt and pepper, then squeeze over lime juice.

Serve with the lime dipping sauce. Make sure you don't eat the lemongrass sticks!

PETE'S SNAPPER SLIDERS

WITH SALSA VERDE

These very thin Vogel's sliders, came about from an impromptu party and the need to make my freshly caught snapper go a little further. They ended up stealing the show, so here they are to share.

Peter Young

SERVES: 32 | PREP: 20 MINS | COOK: 10 MINS | DIFFICULTY: EASY

8 slices very thin Vogel's bread

3 Tbsp olive oil

Mayonnaise

1 snapper, filleted, skin on

Sea salt and pepper

SALSA VERDE:

1 green capsicum, deseeded and finely chopped

¼ cup shallots, finely diced

½ Tbsp minced garlic

2 Tbsp minced capers

⅓ cup gherkins, finely diced

⅓ cup parsley, finely chopped

¼ cup fresh mint, finely chopped

¼ cup fresh basil, finely chopped

1 Tbsp tarragon, finely chopped

Zest of 1 lemon

2 Tbsp lemon juice

½ cup olive oil (lemon infused optional)

½ Tbsp sugar

Ground pepper and sea salt

Prepare and assemble all ingredients before cooking the snapper as the sliders need to be constructed straight after the fish is cooked. You can use the fish collars and wings as well.

To make the salsa verde, combine all the salsa ingredients into a large bowl and refrigerate for half a day, stirring occasionally to help blend and combine all the flavours.

Take 8 slices of Vogel's bread, remove the crusts, then cut into quarters.

Put on an oven tray, brush lightly with olive oil and grill until crisp and golden.

Turn the bread over, oil and grill the other side then leave to cool (toasting can be done several hours before).

Lay the toasted bread on a platter and apply a generous layer of mayonnaise. Season the snapper fillets with sea salt and pepper.

Add a little oil and butter to a medium pan and cook the snapper (skin side first) until just cooked through, then remove.

Cut the snapper into small portions and place on top of the bread (skin side up), drizzle a teaspoon of the salsa verde on top of the snapper, season with salt and pepper and add a squeeze of lemon juice.

Serve immediately.

Notes: Thanks to Al Brown for the salsa recipe.

Homemade aioli could be used as an alternative to mayonnaise.

Phuong Graham

ROLL ON UP

Phuong Graham was happily carving out a successful career in the Blenheim wine industry in 2004, when her husband James was offered a job at a winery close to her favourite childhood holiday spot: Whangateau. 'I'd always wanted to live here,' says Phuong.

The move was followed swiftly by pregnancy, prompting Phuong to rethink her work as a food technician. 'I wanted to keep doing something I enjoyed, but I really wanted to be at home with our son.'

Opportunity presented itself in the newly opened Matakana Farmers' Market. Phuong, who was born in Vietnam but grew up in Auckland, drew on the food of her childhood for inspiration. For her first stall, she lovingly wrapped up 100 rice paper rolls and they disappeared within the hour. 'So the next week, I thought I'd better bring some more,' smiles Phuong.

'We're making homely, authentic Vietnamese food – it's just what I know and love.'

Viet Q Foods has grown over time, with the market stall soon joined by a weekday food truck where she could share the everyday Vietnamese cuisine she was already serving up for friends and family.

Why do people love her food? Phuong shrugs, 'None of it's too fusion. We're making homely, authentic Vietnamese food – it's just what I know and love.'

For Phuong, James and their two boys Thomas and Andrew, creating their own rice paper rolls is a wonderful family occasion.

TAKATU
MATAKANA

FRESH RICE PAPER ROLLS

WITH SHALLOW FRIED FLOUNDER

Rice paper rolls are a fresh and pretty Vietnamese classic, perfect as a canapé, a picnic dish or to pack in a school lunchbox. You can make them a few hours ahead and store them in plastic wrap to be sure they don't dry out.

The Graham Family

SERVES: 6 | PREP: 30 MINS + 30 MINS ROLLING | COOK: 15 MINS | DIFFICULTY: EASY

1 medium sized fresh flounder

1 Tbsp salt

Salt and pepper to season

2 garlic cloves, crushed

Canola oil for frying

DIPPING SAUCE:

¼ cup sugar

¼ cup white vinegar

¼ cup fish sauce

½ tsp garlic, finely chopped

½ tsp birds eye chilli, finely chopped

2 Tbsp freshly squeezed lime juice

RICE PAPER ROLLS:

1 packet rice vermicelli

Platter of herb mix (mint, Vietnamese mint, mesclun salad, fish mint, coriander, purple perilla, watercress)

2 carrots, finely julienned

100g mung bean sprouts

Half red cabbage

1 packet rice papers

Freshen flounder by rubbing with 1 tablespoon of salt and rinsing under cold water then pat dry. Season by sprinkling with 1 teaspoon of salt, ½ teaspoon of pepper and rub with 2 cloves of finely crushed garlic. Leave to marinate for 10-20 minutes.

Heat oil to a medium heat, gently place flounder in the oil to fry for 5-7 minutes on one side, then carefully turn over and fry for another 5-7 minutes until both sides are golden and the edges are crispy. Drain on paper towels when cooked.

Combine all ingredients for the dipping sauce.

For the rice paper rolls, bring a big pot of water to the boil, place 1 packet of vermicelli in the water and push down to soak all vermicelli. Turn off the heat, replace lid and leave for 10 minutes. Then put the vermicelli into a colander, rinse under cold water and drain until ready to use. Wash all herbs, spin dry and arrange on a big platter. Finely julienne carrots and place on a separate platter with mung bean sprouts.

Place half a red cabbage on a flat plate and use 2 bamboo chopsticks to hold the fish upright to display beautifully. Using a sharp knife, split each chopstick half way down the length, push chopsticks into the half cabbage, then carefully place the fried flounder in between the splits of the chopsticks.

Place all ingredients including; fish, herb platter, carrot and mung bean sprout platter, dipping sauce, plates and small bowls for the sauce on the table. Also have a bowl of lukewarm water on the table for dipping rice papers in before rolling.

Dip rice paper into the water to wet completely then shake off excess water. Place onto a plate and put a small amount of vermicelli, carrot, mung bean sprouts, herbs and fish onto the paper. Roll from the bottom of the rice paper, over the roll fillings, fold in both sides and complete rolling over to seal the rice paper roll.

Continue to roll until all ingredients are used up. Dip rolls in dipping sauce and enjoy.

PORK DUMPLINGS

We make this recipe for our family. It's quick and we can make it with our hands. The vegetables just blend in...they are fun to make, fun to cook and fun to eat! Aunty Nat taught us to make them.

Stirling, George and Beau Sutherland

SERVES: 5 | PREP: 10 MINS | COOK: 5 MINS | DIFFICULTY: EASY

500g pork mince

3 carrots, grated

2 spring onions, finely sliced

Block of firm tofu (optional)

Herbs (coriander, mint, Vietnamese mint), chopped

2 tsp sesame oil

1 Tbsp soy sauce

1 packet fresh dumpling wrappers

Mix the mince, grated carrots, spring onions, tofu (if using), herbs, sesame oil and soy sauce with your hands.

Have a small bowl of water nearby.

Take a dumpling wrapper and lay it on the flat of your palm. Put in a large teaspoonful of mixture (not too much as the dumpling won't close properly), dip your finger into the water and run it around the edge of the wrapper, then fold it over in half covering the mixture.

Pinch the edge of the wrapper to close it.

Put the dumpling into a lightly greased steamer or onto baking paper inside a steamer (bamboo or stainless steel is fine).

Fill the steamer up with the dumplings (not touching each other) and set it over a pot of boiling water. Cook for approximately 5 minutes.

Eat them hot served with soy or tamari sauce with chilli added.

Notes: You can also fry them a little after they are steamed to make them crispy.

Phil Armstrong & Annie Wills

BUFFALO DREAMING

Growing up on the family farm, Phil Armstrong never pictured a future in the milking shed. 'I enjoyed dairy farming so much that I spent the next 17 years on fishing boats,' he laughs.

Then he met his wife, Waikato-born Annie Wills. After travelling through Europe and Mozambique (where they contemplated starting a fishing business), the couple kept thinking about the water buffalo farms they had seen in Italy.

'I couldn't believe buffalo were farmed in Italy and Germany, but not in New Zealand – a world leader in livestock farming,' says Phil.

> ***'I couldn't believe buffalo were farmed in Italy and Germany, but not in New Zealand'***

Annie, who has a degree in agriculture, began researching buffalo and the pair teamed up with her parents to purchase a 50-acre farm in the Whangaripo Valley. 'Buffalo milk has a higher [monetary] value than dairy milk,' says Phil. 'We felt it could still be a viable business, even on a smaller property.'

The farm may have been small, but their vision was growing bigger and before long they were exploring other uses for the calcium-rich milk. Annie and Pam went off to study cheesemaking and soon after, the Whangaripo Buffalo Cheese Company was born.

The business has since expanded to include a cheese factory and additional grazing, but it's still a family affair. The company's signature cheeses Marin Blue and St Malo, are named for Annie and Phil's two sons Marin and Malo, both of whom help out in the factory and on the farm.

Labneh is Phil's favourite soft cheese, best made with thick and creamy buffalo yoghurt and paired with Himalayan rock salt. 'It's fantastic on a ham sandwich.'

LABNEH BALLS

Labneh is a tasty and satisfying soft cheese that is easy to make at home. Spread it on crackers, serve it with crusty bread, or roll it into balls and marinate it in olive oil. A delicious addition to any tasting plate or platter.

Phil Armstrong & Annie Wills

SERVES: 500 GRAMS (APPROX) | PREP: 24-48 HOURS | NO COOKING | DIFFICULTY: BASIC

1kg buffalo yoghurt (or Greek yoghurt)

1 garlic clove, crushed

1½ tsp sea salt

Muslin (at least 50cm square)

Fresh (or dried) herbs e.g. parsley, rosemary or Italian herbs, finely chopped

Lemon zest

Olive oil

Combine yoghurt, garlic and salt and mix well.

Line a colander or sieve with the muslin and spoon in the yoghurt mixture. Tie up the muslin to create a ball.

Suspend over a container (in the colander or tied to a wooden spoon) to catch the whey and place in the fridge for 24-48 hours.

Take walnut sized pieces of the soft cheese and roll into balls then roll the balls in the bowl of herbs.

Place cheese balls and lemon in a clean jar with olive oil.

Keeps in a sealed jar in the fridge for up to 2 weeks.

Delwyn Ward

THE UNEXPECTED BREWER

Delwyn Ward seems almost surprised to find herself at the heart of successful kombucha brand, Daily Organics.

Delwyn and her family had been selling fresh smoothies at the Matakana Village Farmers' Market for years, when they decided to throw in some kombucha, a lightly effervescent sweetened tea, fermented with a symbiotic culture of bacteria and yeast.

'I was just tra-la-la-ing with kombucha at the market, using recycled Grolsch bottles, with handmade labels,' smiles Delwyn. 'And then the Ministry for Primary Industries called.'

Suddenly faced with a dizzying array of compliance requirements, Delwyn realised she had two options: game over or game on.

'We've always been into being green and sustainable'

So began months of work: ensuring compliance with organic production standards to gain Biogro certification, finding commercial premises and establishing the nutritional content of the kombucha.

Daily Organics finally launched at the Farmers' Market in May 2014. Within a year, Delwyn was joined at the helm by business partner Brad Gwynne, who she met at the market. 'His systems focus is a great balance to my creativity.'

Has it all been smooth sailing? 'Well, no. You have to have a certain amount of bloody mindedness. Or naivety. Some days you don't know if you're really ballsy or really stupid to push on.'

Making a 'magical' product – a raw, living, organic-certified thing – means the world to Delwyn. 'We've always been into being green and sustainable. I suppose we are hippies really.'

Delwyn is relishing building a business close to her Pakiri home and employing locals. 'I love working with people who went to Mahu College, who live here and have their families here.'

THE VINTRY KOMBUCHA MARTINI

This local twist on a classic Tom Collins was inspired by Delwyn's kombucha, and is perfect for gin lovers, or as a refreshing aperitif in the late afternoon sun. The Kombucha Martini has a savoury finish, so usually suits a more discerning drinker: Think George Clooney rather than Justin Bieber.

Raj Bhalla, The Vintry

SERVES: 1 | PREP: 5 MINS | NO COOKING | DIFFICULTY: BASIC

45ml Scapegrace Gin (or any good quality dry gin)

15ml Chase Elderflower Liqueur

Juice of ½ fresh lemon

90ml Daily Organics Original Kombucha

Slivered lemon zest

A slice of lemon (optional)

Take a chilled martini glass. Rub the edge of the glass with a good sliver of lemon zest.

Place gin, elderflower liqueur and lemon juice in a cocktail shaker.

Shake over ice. Strain and pour into the chilled martini glass.

Top up with kombucha.

Float lemon zest on top and garnish with a slice of lemon.

THAI FISH CAKES

These fresh little works of culinary art are so quick and simple to make and everyone loves them!

From the Kitchen of the Vivian Gallery

SERVES: 6 | PREP: 15 MINS | COOK: 10 MINS | DIFFICULTY: BASIC

450g fish fillets (white-fleshed such as cod)

3 Tbsp coconut milk

2½ Tbsp fish sauce

½ Tbsp chilli powder

⅓ tsp ground cumin

¼ tsp ground coriander

½ tsp brown sugar

½ cup breadcrumbs

6 kaffir lime leaves, cut into thin strips or ½ tsp lime zest, grated

2 green onions, thinly sliced

1 galangal, grated or thumb-sized piece ginger, grated

3 garlic cloves

1 red chilli, minced or ¼ tsp dried crushed chilli

1 to 2 Tbsp oil for high temperature frying (such as peanut oil)

Handful of fresh coriander

Lime wedges

Cucumber, chopped

Thai sweet chili sauce

Rinse fish and pat dry thoroughly. Cut into chunks and place in a food processor.

In a small bowl or measuring cup, combine the coconut milk, fish sauce, chilli powder, cumin, coriander and brown sugar. Stir with a fork to combine, then pour into the food processor over the fish.

Add breadcrumbs, kaffir lime leaves, green onion, galangal (or ginger), garlic and chilli. Pulse to combine. You should be able to pick this mixture up in your hand and form it into cakes. If you find it too wet, add more breadcrumbs and pulse again until you get a good consistency. (Much of this will depend on the fish you're using and how much moisture it contains).

Scoop up a small amount in your hand - about the size of a golf ball - and pat into a small cake and set on a clean plate. Note that traditional Thai fish cakes are small and not too thick (about 5cm in diameter and 2-2.5cm thick).

It helps to rinse your hands after making each cake.

Place fish cakes in the refrigerator for 10 minutes to firm up. Meanwhile, pour oil into a small frying pan or wok, at least 2.5cm deep, and prepare your garnishes.

Heat oil. When it is hot enough - a breadcrumb should sizzle and cook immediately when dropped in - gently set cakes in the oil.

Fry for approximately 30-60 seconds before turning, gently lifting cakes from the bottom of the pan. Fry until golden brown and drain on a paper towel.

Top with fresh coriander and serve with lime wedges, squeezed over just before eating along with cucumber and Thai sweet chili sauce on the side for dipping.

Notes: You can make the fish paste up to 24 hours in advance. Cover and set in the refrigerator, then form into cakes and fry right before eating.

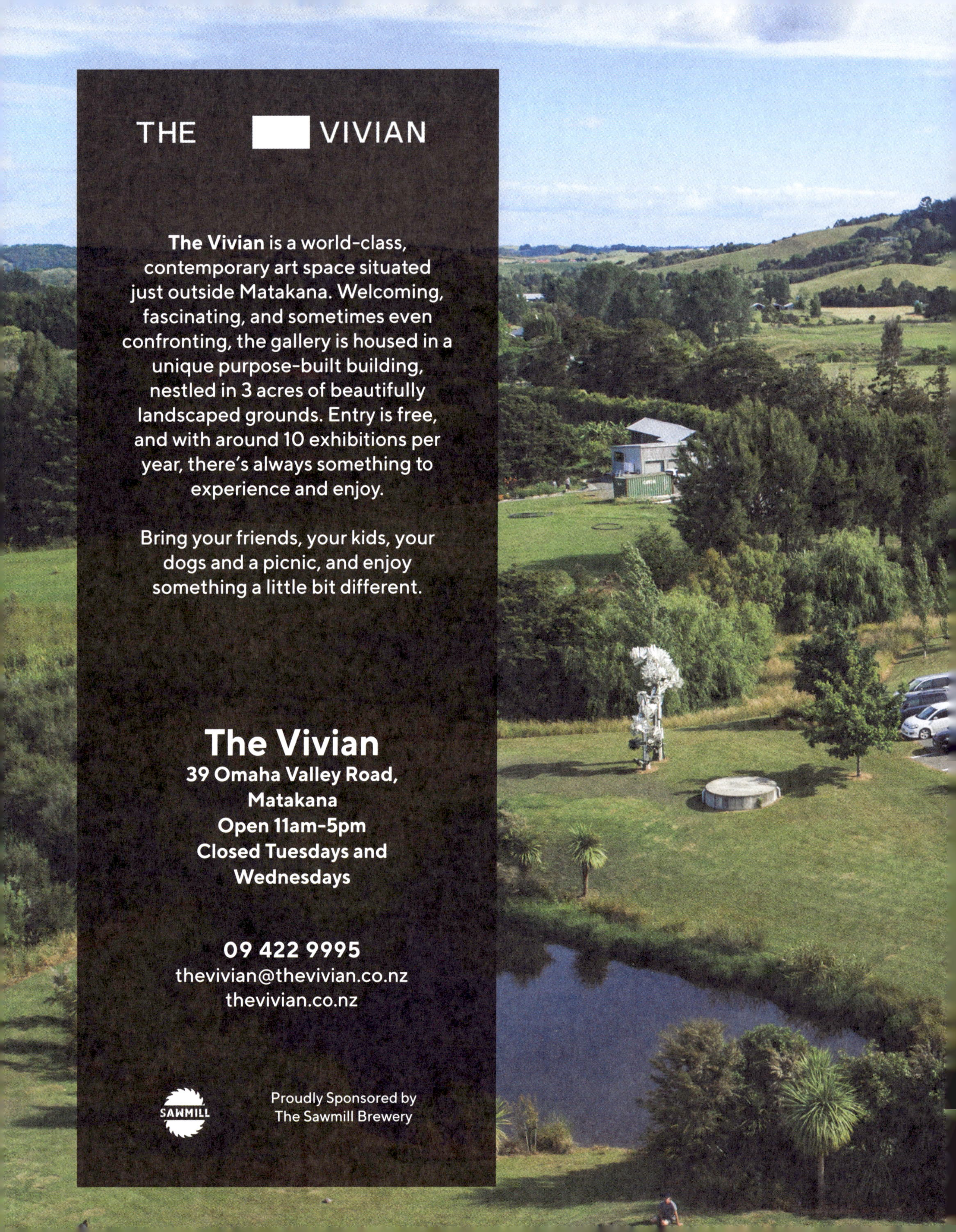
THE VIVIAN
The Vivian is a world-class, contemporary art space situated just outside Matakana. Welcoming, fascinating, and sometimes even confronting, the gallery is housed in a unique purpose-built building, nestled in 3 acres of beautifully landscaped grounds. Entry is free, and with around 10 exhibitions per year, there's always something to experience and enjoy.
Bring your friends, your kids, your dogs and a picnic, and enjoy something a little bit different.
The Vivian
39 Omaha Valley Road, Matakana
Open 11am-5pm
Closed Tuesdays and Wednesdays
09 422 9995
thevivian@thevivian.co.nz
thevivian.co.nz
SAWMILL
Proudly Sponsored by The Sawmill Brewery

Light Meals

The Green Swap, Matakana Wharf

Every Friday in summer, and monthly in winter, a group of keen gardeners meet to exchange the fruits (and veggies) of their labour at the Matakana Green Swap.

If your garden is overtaken by kale or pumpkins, or your trees are laden with plums or feijoas, why not trade your excess for a jar of home-made lemon curd or freshly gathered watercress?

There's plenty of haggling and even outbidding ('I'll see your worm tea and raise you one bag of firewood'), but it's all in good fun and everyone goes home satisfied.

It's a chance to catch up with friends and neighbours, and gather inspiration for the garden or the table. We hope this chapter gives you a few ideas on how to deal with your bounty.

ASIAN NOODLE SALAD

This Asian salad recipe is so easy to throw together and is full of flavours. It works great prepared in advance as well.

Jude Orr

SERVES: 6 | PREP: 10 MINS | COOK: 5 MINS | DIFFICULTY: BASIC

250g rice stick noodles

2 cups fresh green beans (or frozen)

2 cups shredded chicken

½ cup roasted peanuts, roughly chopped

3 Tbsp coriander, roughly chopped

1 Tbsp sesame seeds, toasted

2 cups bean sprouts

½ tsp salt

Ground black pepper

Lime wedges to serve

DRESSING:

1 Tbsp sesame oil

2 Tbsp canola oil (or other neutral oil)

2 tsp fish sauce

Boil some water in a large pot and add the rice noodles.

Leave for 1 minute then remove from the heat and allow to cool for 10 minutes or longer.

Drain the noodles and rinse under cold water.

Prepare the beans, trimming the ends and boil them in salted water for 5 minutes.

Drain the beans and rinse in cold water.

Mix the noodles, beans and shredded chicken together in a large serving bowl with the roasted peanuts, coriander, sesame seeds and bean sprouts.

For the dressing, put the sesame oil, canola oil and fish sauce in a mug and mix together.

Combine the dressing through the noodle salad and add salt and pepper.

Serve as a salad at room temperature or mix in a hot pan for 2-3 minutes for a stir fry side dish.

Decorate with lime wedges when you serve.

Notes: If you don't have green beans, you can use peas instead. Also, if you're vegetarian, omit the chicken.

SWEET & SAVOURY CHICKPEA SALAD

This is a very popular salad. Every time I have made it for our friends and family, I have been asked for the recipe!

The Macky Family

SERVES: 5 | PREP: 30 MINS | COOK: 5 MINS | DIFFICULTY: BASIC

800g chickpeas, rinsed, drained

1 large carrot, peeled, grated

1 cup boiled green beans (fresh or frozen)

⅓ cup dates, diced

1 tsp ground cumin

1 tsp ground turmeric

2 tsp honey

1 tsp lemon zest

3 Tbsp lemon juice

¼ cup freshly squeezed orange juice

¼ cup olive oil

½ tsp fresh chilli, chopped (optional)

Pinch of salt

¼ cup parsley or coriander (or both), chopped

Place the chickpeas in a bowl and add the carrot, green beans, dates, cumin, turmeric, honey, lemon zest, citrus juice, olive oil, chilli and salt. Then toss well to combine all the ingredients.

Taste and adjust the seasoning if needed and leave to marinate in the fridge for at least an hour.

When ready to serve, add the fresh parsley and coriander.

Kerri Johns & Sarah Willis

THE SWEET & THE SAVOURY

On first meeting, Sarah Willis and Kerri Johns didn't know they shared a passion for culinary creations.

Sarah worked in banking and enjoyed making beautiful food for friends, family and children's parties. Kerri was a physiotherapist whose creative outlet was cooking.

'We're very similar but we're also quite different,' laughs Kerri. 'Even in the kitchen Sarah is sweet focused and I'm savoury.'

The two friends were both keen to find employment that would accommodate the needs of their young children, so in 2014 they purchased a mobile kitchen and launched their catering business - Ravish. 'We took a leap of faith there would be work to do' says Kerri.

Word quickly spread and the mobile kitchen was soon followed by The Kiosk. The pair transformed a rustic shed on a busy corner site into a thriving coffee stop with open air bench seating, serving decadent slices, scones and salads. Within three months, they were both working full-time in the business.

'Cooking is love personified '

'Some locals come in three times a day,' says Sarah. 'Before I bake, I ask people at the counter, "What do you feel like?" They come in a few days later and it's there.'

That freedom to enjoy such a close connection with their customers means Sarah and Kerri never get bored. 'When we know people are having a tough time, we can openly or discreetly help them with meals or lunch box things.'

'Cooking is love personified,' says Sarah, 'I love that saying. So this is love with cream cheese icing!' The two friends laugh. 'And Kerri's would be like love with balsamic dressing!'

WALNUT, FENNEL & PINK GRAPEFRUIT SALAD

A popular refreshing salad that goes great with salmon or lamb.

Sarah & Kerri

SERVES: 4-6 | PREP: 30 MINS | COOK: 20 MINS | DIFFICULTY: EASY

1 medium fennel bulb with fronds
2 Tbsp honey
Drizzle of olive oil
Flaky salt
1 pink grapefruit (or use regular grapefruit, oranges or pomegranate)

DRESSING:
⅓ cup grapefruit juice
2 Tbsp white wine vinegar
½ cup olive oil
½ tsp Dijon mustard
½ tsp honey
Salt and pepper

CANDIED WALNUTS:
⅓ cup caster sugar
1 Tbsp honey
¼ cup cold water
1 tsp chilli flakes
1 cup walnuts
1 packet rocket

Preheat oven to 180°C. Mandolin or thinly slice the fennel. Keep fronds aside. Put cut fennel on baking paper and drizzle over 2 tablespoons of honey, olive oil and flaky salt. Roast for about 15-20 minutes. Cut segments of pink grapefruit. Reserve juice for the dressing. To make the dressing, mix grapefruit juice, white wine vinegar, olive oil, Dijon mustard, honey, salt and pepper.

For the candied walnuts, combine sugar, honey and cold water in a pot over a low heat. Cook, stirring for 5 minutes or until sugar has dissolved. Increase heat to high and bring to the boil. Boil, without stirring, for 5-7 minutes or until mixture turns light golden in colour. Remove from heat and quickly add the chilli and walnuts. Stir to combine. Spread nut mixture over prepared tray. Bake for 5-7 minutes or until mixture bubbles and nuts are golden. Remove from oven. Cool on tray. Once cool, using hands, break up nut clusters.

To assemble, put rocket on a platter, place fennel and grapefruit segments on top and drizzle with dressing. Then place the candied walnuts on top of the salad and decorate with fennel fronds.

Explore the wine trail or grab a light snack and coffee

CHICKPEA FARINATA BREAD

This has to be the easiest, tastiest and most filling 'bread' to make. I usually make it as a side with soup in winter, but it is just as delicious served with dips and antipasto.

Juliana Cowen

SERVES: 10 SLICES | PREP: 10 MINS | COOK: 15-20 MINS | DIFFICULTY: BASIC

1 cup warm water

1 cup chickpea flour

1 tsp salt

1 tsp black pepper

1-2 tsp ground cumin

1½-2 tsp olive oil

1 onion, thinly sliced (optional)

Black sesame seeds (optional)

Fresh rosemary (optional)

Preheat oven to 220°C.

Oil a 23cm round pan with cooking spray.

Mix all of the ingredients in a bowl, except sesame seeds and rosemary. Pour into the pan and bake for 15-20 minutes.

Slice bread into wedges, top with the sesame seeds and rosemary and put under the grill.

Serve warm.

CHRISTMAS COUSCOUS SALAD

This recipe was inspired by a salad that I used to buy from one of my favourite salad bars that closed down. It is popular among friends and asked for on a regular basis - colourful, simple, fresh and easy.

Kim McKergow

SERVES: 10 | PREP: 10 MINS | COOK: 10 MINS | DIFFICULTY: BASIC

1 cup Israeli couscous

70g pine nuts

1 pomegranate, seeds

¼ cup parsley, finely chopped

½ cup cranberries, dried

Handful of mixed seeds or nuts

1 Tbsp balsamic vinegar

2-3 Tbsp extra virgin olive oil

Salt and cracked pepper to taste

Boil a pot of water with a teaspoon of oil. Once boiled add the couscous and cook until the couscous is al dente (approximately 8 minutes). Drain and rinse with cold water.

Brown the pine nuts in a pan.

Mix in a salad bowl with all other ingredients.

Add salt and pepper to taste.

Notes: Keep an eye on the pine nuts to avoid burning as they continue to cook once they are off the heat.

Wendy Inger

FALLING IN LOVE WITH AVOCADOS

As a young woman, Wendy Inger couldn't stand avocados.

Every time she visited her parents at their Omokoroa orchard, they would send her back to the city with a bag of the jolly things. So she kept trying to acquire the taste, and eventually hit on a winner when she teamed sliced avocado with marmite on toast.

That humble brekkie was the start of a new love affair. 'Now, if I don't eat an avocado every day, I miss it,' says Wendy. 'Avocados are so good for you and have a beautiful flavour. I love them with eggs for breakfast.'

> *'We wanted to plant something that we loved to eat'*

When Wendy and her husband Garry purchased a block of land in the fertile Omaha Flats in 2000, avocados were the obvious crop of choice.

'We wanted to plant something that we loved to eat,' says Wendy. 'But everyone said avocados wouldn't work, because the peat soil would give them wet feet.'

The couple decided to plant two avocado trees as a trial, mounding up the earth to keep the roots aerated. They also planted 3,000 tamarillo trees, but these turned out to be hard work for little reward, and after six years, Wendy felt 'quite happy' when a storm took out the lot.

Meanwhile, the two avocado trees were flourishing and have since been joined by 80 more. Their thriving roadside stall on the road to Omaha is a regular stop for many and sees the couple picking and packing as many as 40 to 50 bags per day on busy summer weekends.

With such heavily laden trees, Wendy continues to enjoy experimenting with different ways to relish this nourishing and versatile fruit.

Three Ways with Avocado

Avocado smoothie - For a rich creamy texture with less sugar, replace the banana in your morning smoothie with one quarter of a ripe avocado.

Avocado dressing - Blend together one ripe avocado, 1 cup of fresh orange juice, ½ cup of lime juice, 4 tablespoons of honey and a pinch of salt.

Blend until smooth and use this hearty dressing in place of a vinaigrette.

Smashed avocado - Cube an avocado and place it into a mixing bowl. Add 80g of feta, chopped mint, finely chopped chilli (with seeds if you like the heat) and the juice of 1 lime.

Use a fork to combine into a paste. Toast your favourite bread, spoon the avocado mixture onto the toast and add a sprig of mint as garnish.

This is delicious served with a poached egg on top and a side of crispy bacon!

Brick Bay

WINTER SALAD WITH CREAMY CASHEW
& PRESERVED LEMON DRESSING

Here is a colourful, warming, hearty salad for colder months. The sweetness of the squash goes beautifully with the sharpness and creaminess of the preserved lemon dressing. Preserved lemons are lacto-fermented, so they contain loads of naturally occurring probiotics to give your immune system a boost, just when it is most needed during the shorter days of autumn and winter, which is also when squash are in season.

Amber Rose

SERVES: 4-6 | PREP: 30 MINS + SOAKING | COOK: 40 MINS | DIFFICULTY: MEDIUM

1 large butternut squash (or pumpkin)

4 Tbsp ghee or olive oil

1 Tbsp sunflower seeds

1 Tbsp pumpkin seeds

1 Tbsp black sesame seeds

10g flaked almonds

10g basil leaves

Handful of rocket

Pomegranate, seeds removed and rinsed

Extra virgin olive oil

Sea salt and freshly ground black pepper

CASHEW & PRESERVED LEMON DRESSING:

150g cashews, soaked for 4 hours or overnight

2 Tbsp preserved lemons, chopped

1 crushed garlic clove

200ml almond milk

Sea salt and freshly ground black pepper

Preheat the oven to 220°C.

Trim the base and top off the squash, then cut it in half lengthways. Use a spoon to remove the seeds. Cut each half into wedges about 3cm thick.

Arrange the wedges on a roasting tray, skin side down. Brush with ghee or olive oil and season well with salt and pepper. Roast for 30-35 minutes. Keep an eye on the wedges – depending on your oven they may take a little longer or a little less, but you don't want them to burn.

To make the dressing simply put all the ingredients into a bowl and blitz with a stick blender, adding more almond milk if you require a thinner consistency for drizzling, or less for a dip. Season to taste and set aside while you prepare the salad.

When the wedges are just catching at the edges and feel tender all the way through when poked with a knife, remove from the oven and allow to cool.

Reduce the oven temperature to 180°C and put all the seeds and the almonds onto a clean baking tray. Pop into the oven to toast for 6-8 minutes, or until lightly browned and popping.

When you are ready to assemble the salad, arrange the squash on a beautiful serving platter, sprinkle over the toasted seeds, almonds, basil, rocket and pomegranate seeds, then serve with the dressing on the side.

As a final flourish you can drizzle with extra virgin olive oil and add an extra sprinkle of sea salt and freshly ground black pepper.

HEALTHY SEED LOAF

Incredibly satisfying and a wonderfully healthy alternative to bread.

Philippa Emanuel

SERVES: 8 | PREP: 10 MINS | COOK: 50 MINS | DIFFICULTY: EASY

- **1½ cups rolled oats**
- **1 cup sunflower seeds or mix with pumpkin seeds**
- **½ cup flax seeds**
- **2 Tbsp chia seeds**
- **4 Tbsp psyllium husk**
- **1 tsp salt**
- **½ cup almonds or cashews (optional)**
- **2 Tbsp melted coconut oil**
- **1 cup water**
- **2 Tbsp maple syrup (optional)**

Preheat oven to 170°C.

Put all ingredients in a bowl and gently mix.

Pour into a lined loaf tin and let it bind together for a minimum of 2 hours - the longer the better.

Place in the oven for 30 minutes.

Remove from the oven and turn loaf upside down on the oven rack. Place back in the oven at the same temperature for 20-25 minutes - it should be slightly browned and firm.

CURRIED PARSNIP & PEAR SOUP

This soup is a real winner, especially with the kids. It's our go-to winter-warmer to satisfy hungry little tums after swimming practice or after a wild windy walk along the beach. It's based on a recipe from Ripe Recipes, a cookbook published by the Ripe Deli.

Dave Hassan

SERVES: 4 | PREP: 10 MINS | COOK: 30-40 MINS | DIFFICULTY: BASIC

1 Tbsp olive oil
1 onion
2 garlic cloves, crushed
1 tsp mustard seeds
1 tsp ground cumin
1 tsp fresh ginger, peeled, finely chopped
1 Tbsp curry powder
4 large parsnips, chopped
1 kumara (optional), chopped
2 pears, chopped
4 cups vegetable or chicken stock
1 Tbsp soft brown sugar
1 Tbsp butter
¼ cup cream

Heat oil over medium heat. Sauté onion and garlic for 2 minutes.

Add mustard seeds, cumin, ginger and curry powder and cook for a further 2 minutes, stirring so they don't burn.

Add parsnips, kumara (if using), pears and stock.

Stir to combine. Cook for approximately 30 minutes until vegetables are soft.

Stir through brown sugar, butter and cream and cook for a few more minutes.

Blend with a stick blender until smooth. Season with salt and pepper to taste.

Notes: You can substitute apple for pear.

Ruth Soriano Andaluz

A TASTE OF SPAIN

After emigrating from Spain to Matakana in 2015, with her husband Eduardo Abellan and children Leonardo and Judith, Ruth Soriano Andaluz found her niche teaching Spanish to local children. Her classes were so successful that Ruth was inspired to share more of her Spanish culture with the local community.

And what better way to do this than by sharing Spain's most popular (and coldest) vegetable soup?

'Kiwis are actually very adventurous when it comes to food'

'In Spain, we always find ways to make good use of our spare vegetables,' says Ruth. And because Spain has so many big and juicy tomatoes in summer, the perfect gazpacho is always there for the making.

All gazpacho ingredients are diced and sprinkled onto separate plates, so each diner can create the perfect soup for their individual tastes. You can serve it as an entrée, eat it as a soup or drink it as a smoothie - and it's extra delicious with croutons.

Ruth's gazpacho is a huge hit with her New Zealand friends, who you'll often find perched outside her home on hot summer days, soup bowl in hand. 'I think Kiwis are actually very adventurous when it comes to food, and you all seem to love vegetables.'

Ruth, Eduardo, Leonardo and Judith are thrilled with life in Matakana. 'It's so relaxing here,' says Ruth. 'Even more so with a good gazpacho.'

GAZPACHO ANDALUZ

Gazpacho is a traditional summer dish from Andalusia in Spain. Mostly known now for being served cold, the gazpacho has many different influences from Greece and Rome, but also from the Moorish and Arab cultures. We love having a refreshing gazpacho on a hot summer's day - it's a delicious way to eat more veggies!

Abellan Soriano Family

SERVES: 4-6 | PREP: 15 MINS | NO COOKING | DIFFICULTY: EASY

- **10 ripe tomatoes, chopped**
- **½ onion, chopped**
- **1 slice bread (use gluten free if preferred)**
- **½ medium telegraph cucumber, peeled and chopped**
- **½ medium green & red capsicum, chopped**
- **1 short stick celery**
- **1 garlic clove, crushed**
- **1 cup water**
- **2 Tbsp vinegar**
- **Spanish extra-virgin olive oil**
- **Salt and pepper**
- **Croutons**

In a food processor combine tomatoes, onion, bread, cucumber, capsicum, celery, garlic, water and vinegar until the mixture becomes a thick orange liquid.

Taste for acidity; this will vary with the sweetness of the tomatoes, if it is not acidic enough, add a little more vinegar. Add the extra-virgin olive oil, season with salt and blend again.

Strain the gazpacho into a jar and refrigerate for at least half an hour.

Serve the gazpacho (when it is refreshingly chilled) in a soup plate or bowl, topped with a little olive oil, the desired chopped vegetables, croutons and jamón serrano.

If the gazpacho is too liquid you can add more bread.

To make ahead, refrigerate blended gazpacho for up to 3 days; stir well before serving.

HEARTY CARROT & CORIANDER SOUP

This vibrant coloured, silky soup has been a family favourite, most often served on cold winter mornings after Saturday sports.

The Barnett Family

SERVES: 4-6 | PREP: 15 MINS | COOK: 25 MINS | DIFFICULTY: EASY

25g butter

1 medium onion, finely chopped

1 garlic clove, crushed

550g carrots, roughly chopped

1 litre vegetable stock

Generous pinch of ground nutmeg

2 Tbsp fresh coriander, roughly chopped

150ml single cream

Salt and pepper to taste

150ml yoghurt or cream

Handful of coriander

Melt the butter and gently cook onion and garlic (do not brown).

Add roughly chopped carrots, stock and nutmeg. Cover, bring to the boil and simmer for approximately 10 minutes, or until vegetables are tender.

Cool, then puree with a stick blender or food processor. Return to a fresh pan, stir in cream and chopped coriander. Add salt and pepper to taste.

Serve garnished with a swirl of cream or yoghurt, coriander and crusty bread and butter on the side.

Notes: Chicken stock can be used in place of vegetable stock. For a more textured soup, grate 100g of the 550g carrots and add it raw to the pan after blending.

TOM'S COCONUT LENTIL SOUP

This is our son Tom's favourite winter lunch, brought to school in a mini thermos. It can be made from mostly dry and tinned ingredients, so it's a handy recipe when friends call in unexpectedly and the fridge is empty!

The Ward Family

SERVES: 6 | PREP: 10 MINS | COOK: 40 MINS | DIFFICULTY: EASY

1½ Tbsp cumin seeds
1 Tbsp coriander seeds
2 Tbsp olive oil
1 onion, finely chopped
1 cup red lentils
5 cups vegetable stock or water
400ml coconut milk
2 Tbsp fresh ginger, grated
Salt and pepper
Zest of 1 lemon
Juice of 1-2 lemons
Fresh coriander

Toast the cumin and coriander seeds in a heavy-based pan for a few minutes, until you can smell the flavours of the spices.

Don't let them burn.

Add olive oil and the onion, and stir until the onion is clear.

Add lentils, vegetable stock, coconut milk, grated ginger, salt and pepper. Stir well.

Cover and cook on low heat for 35 minutes until lentils have softened and lost shape.

Add additional stock or water if required.

Serve with fresh coriander.

The Sculpture Trail, Brick Bay

Bernadette Hogg

BEAUTY IN THE WEEDS

Appearances can be deceiving in Bernadette Hogg's garden.

That rocket that has gone to seed and that old speckled basil plant might look like evidence of a busy gardener's neglect, but they're actually destined for a supporting role in a future magazine spread.

'When I look at the garden I think about multi-dimensional styling,' says the well-known food writer and stylist, whose work regularly appears in NZ House and Garden magazine. 'I look at flowers and herbs for food styling and as flavours for cocktails, soda syrup, kombucha and tea.'

'There's an amazing community of creative people who love and are inspired by food'

Bernadette has been digging up Matakana soil since 2000, when she, her husband Peter and their three young children traded city life for five acres on the Glen Eden River.

'We wanted to live on the land and let our kids experience the freedom of space, but everyone just thought we were having a midlife crisis,' she laughs.

If it was a crisis, it was a particularly savvy one for this professional foodie: Matakana was about to become known as an artisanal food and viticultural destination.

'When we first arrived there were sturdy lettuces and seasonal produce, but there wasn't the variety. When the market began it was hugely exciting - now I can go from stall to stall and gather everything I need. There's an amazing community of people who love and are inspired by food.'

ASPARAGUS & PANCETTA QUICHE

This simple quiche recipe is a favourite of mine and is pretty much fail proof even for those who are pastry shy. The flavours can vary based on whichever seasonal ingredients are in abundance or whatever is left in the fridge at the end of the week.

Bernadette Hogg

SERVES: 6 | PREP: 30 MINS | COOK: 45 MINS | DIFFICULTY: MEDIUM

PASTRY:

200g flour

100g butter, well chilled, cut into small cubes

1 egg yolk

3-4 Tbsp chilled water

FILLING:

20g butter

1 small onion, finely chopped

8 slices pancetta, roughly chopped

30g gruyere cheese, grated

3 eggs

150ml cream

50ml milk

Zest of small lemon, finely grated

Pinch of nutmeg, freshly grated

Salt and pepper

450g fresh asparagus, ends trimmed, blanched

Preheat oven to 190°C.

To make the pastry, place the flour and butter into the bowl of a food processor. Add the egg yolk and 3-4 tablespoons of chilled water. Continue to process until the pastry comes together in a ball (you may need to add a little extra water).

Form the pastry into a flat brick shape, cover with plastic wrap and refrigerate for at least 30 minutes.

Roll the pastry between two sheets of plastic wrap until large enough to line the tin. Prick the base all over using a fork. Cover the pastry with crumpled baking paper and top with a layer of baking beans. Bake for 10 minutes then remove from the oven and take out the paper and beans. Trim the pastry edges and return the pastry to the oven for a further 5 minutes or until lightly golden.

Reduce the oven temperature to 180°C.

Make the filling by melting the butter in a pan over a low heat, add the onion and half the pancetta, sauté until the onion is soft and transparent. Spoon the mixture over the base of the pastry case and sprinkle with half the cheese.

Mix together the eggs, cream, milk, zest and nutmeg, season with salt and freshly ground black pepper to taste. Pour the mixture into the pastry case and top with the asparagus spears, remaining cheese and slices of pancetta.

Bake for 25-30 minutes until set. Allow to sit for at least 10 minutes before slicing and serving.

Established in 1988,
Matakana Botanicals is
New Zealand's most established
premium body care manufacturer.

Their unique ranges are
inspired by special places around
New Zealand and utilise high
quality locally grown natural 'hero'
ingredients.

Matakana Botanicals
1122 Leigh Road, RD5
Matakana 0985

www.matakanabotanicals.co.nz

MATAKANA BOTANICALS
MADE FROM
NEW ZEALAND

Macadamia &wildfig
Macadamia &wildfig
Macadamia &wildfig

ROASTED FEIJOA & PORK PIZZA

Feijoa and pork roasted together give this amazing fruit a unique sweet and sour flavour. This pizza topped with dollops of Quinta Feijoa chutney will not disappoint!

Helen Lory

SERVES: 2-4 | PREP: 30 MINS | COOK: 2½ HOURS | DIFFICULTY: MEDIUM

Pork shoulder

4 medium feijoas

1 Tbsp olive oil

1 garlic clove, finely chopped

½ small onion or shallot, finely chopped

2 cups cherry tomatoes, halved

1 handful of fresh basil leaves & oregano leaves

Sea salt and freshly ground black pepper to taste

4 store bought thin pizza bases (more adventurous chefs can make their own pizza dough)

1 cup mozzarella cheese, grated

Preheat oven to 160°C.

Slow roast the pork shoulder or loin for 2 hours .

Slice 3-4 medium/large feijoas with skin on into 8-10mm rings and add feijoas to roasting juices for the last 10-15 minutes of cooking. Remove and cool.

For the tomato sauce, sweat down the garlic and onion in 1 tablespoon of olive oil until soft.

Add the cherry tomatoes, basil, oregano, salt and pepper and simmer for 10 minutes or until sauce thickens, then allow to cool.

For the pizza, spread the tomato sauce evenly over the pizza bases. Scatter a thin layer of grated mozzarella cheese over the sauce. Randomly place small pulled pork pieces onto the cheese, place feijoa slices onto the pork. Scatter over another thin layer of grated mozzarella cheese.

Cook in a pizza oven or normal oven at 250°C for 7 minutes until the topping has melted and the pizza base is lightly golden. (Cooking time will be less in a pizza oven).

Notes: It's ideal to have the pork roast the day before as a meal and save 2 cups ready for the pizza!

Brick Bay

James Patterson

FOR THE LOVE OF GOOD FOOD

When it comes to good food, James Patterson has no problem wearing his heart on his sleeve.

His full arm tattoo features detailed images of vegetables and leaves, a tribute to his grandfather's elaborate gardens. 'I have vivid memories of weekends bottling fruit at my grandparents' house,' says James. 'The focus on flavour and seasonality was always there.'

Growing up in such a food-oriented family - his Dad was a baker and now keeps bees, while his sister is a chef - it's no surprise James always planned a career in the kitchen.

After training as a chef, James and then girlfriend Lisa went travelling 'for six months', but didn't come home for nine years. James worked in fine dining establishments across Europe and the UK.

'There's an adrenalin aspect... you do something great and tomorrow you start again'

'I absolutely fell in love with London. But when we had our daughter Emily it was time to come home – the environment we wanted to raise her in was more important than anything.'

Once home, he helped establish a chain of specialty grocers, managing the Matakana store. But the kitchen kept calling. When The Matakana pub was revamped in 2012 James wandered over to 'have a nosey', met the owner and became head chef. 'I missed cooking for people. There's an adrenalin aspect, where you do something great and tomorrow you start again.'

James is proud to have passed on the family love of cooking to Emily and son Christian. 'They both have a great foundation of what makes good food.'

CRAB CAKES WITH AVOCADO DRESSING

Crab is plentiful along our coastline yet often overlooked. Hopefully this delicious, simple recipe will entice a few locals to catch a few fresh crabs themselves and enjoy this decadent seafood.

James Patterson

SERVES: 6 | PREP: 1½ HOURS | COOK: 20 MINS | DIFFICULTY: BASIC

300g crab meat

1 cup fresh breadcrumbs

1 egg, beaten

2 Tbsp mayonnaise

Cracked pepper

1 tsp sweet chilli sauce

Squeeze of lemon juice

Olive oil

AVOCADO DRESSING:

½ ripe avocado

½ cup natural yoghurt

1 Tbsp lemon or lime juice

2 Tbsp sour cream

Combine crab meat with breadcrumbs and mix in beaten egg, mayonnaise, pepper, chilli sauce and lemon juice.

Form into patties and refrigerate for 1 hour to let them set.

Heat oil in a pan over a moderate heat and fry patties lightly until golden on each side, turning once.

For the dressing, combine all ingredients in a food processor until well blended and serve at room temperature.

Serve with a salad, steamed rice and avocado dressing.

Notes: you can also use 150g of crab meat plus 150g of cooked fish.

Christine & Anna Didsbury

ART, WINE & FOOD ENTWINED

Brick Bay Winery is a place of constant evolution. 'We're not driven by trends,' says Anna Didsbury. 'Everything is borne from our passions.'

Over three decades, the Didsburys have transformed their family farm into a boutique vineyard and sculpture trail, with the stunning Glass House restaurant cantilevered over an ever-changing lake.

Love for this land inspired Anna's mother Christine to study viticulture and winemaking in the early 1990s. She planted pinot gris when no one else had heard of it, and as word spread about Brick Bay wine, began considering how to offer a closer connection with the terroir. 'We wanted to give visitors the experience of tasting wine on the land where it is produced,' says Christine. 'That sense of place sets you apart.'

Meanwhile, Anna was studying sculpture at Elam, and later viticulture in Central Otago. She worked a vintage in Burgundy, then met up with her parents, visiting many European sculpture parks where they were inspired by the combination of art and wine. 'Sculpture is often anchored to the landscape,' says Christine, 'While wine speaks of the place. It's about the seasons and creating something special from your terroir.'

An idea began to take shape: An outdoor gallery with sculptures for sale backed by a charitable trust offering artists interest-free loans to create the works. The Didsburys spent many hours walking the land mapping out a trail while architect Noel Lane got to work on a 'tasting shed' that evolved into The Glass House.

Head chef Cameron Cook shares the family's vision of showcasing food produced on the farm: Macadamias, figs, olive oil, honey, veggies and now lamb. 'It's an expression of Brick Bay in a culinary sense,' says Anna.

Brick Bay

Fresh authentic Vietnamese comfort/street food, cooked and served fresh every week, for takeaway from our food truck in Matakana.

Open: Thursday 5-8pm and Friday 11am-8pm and Saturday at the Matakana Village Farmers' Market 8am-1pm

VIETNAMESE SAVOURY PANCAKE

This is one of our most popular specials in the food truck.

From the Kitchen of Viet Q Foods

SERVES: 10-12 PANCAKES | PREP: 45 MINS | COOK: 20-30 MINS | DIFFICULTY: MEDIUM

DIPPING SAUCE:

3 Tbsp sugar

2 Tbsp water

2 Tbsp white vinegar

2 birds eye chillies, finely chopped

2 garlic cloves, finely chopped

5 Tbsp fish sauce

2 Tbsp fresh lime juice

PANCAKE BATTER:

200g rice flour

2 tsp turmeric

400ml coconut milk

250ml coconut water

2 spring onions, finely chopped

½ tsp salt

½ tsp sugar

Canola oil for cooking

1 red onion, thinly sliced

200g pork belly, thinly sliced

400g prawns, shelled, deveined

200g mung bean sprouts

GARNISH & VEGETABLES:

1 head fancy lettuce

1 head cos lettuce

12 leaves mustard greens

Herbs (coriander, cinnamon basil, Vietnamese mint, purple perilla, fish mint)

To make the dipping sauce, dissolve sugar in water and vinegar, add finely chopped chillies and garlic in a bowl, then add fish sauce and lime to taste.

For the pancake batter, mix together flour, turmeric and coconut milk, then add coconut water, spring onions, salt and sugar, making sure the batter is smooth with no lumps.

Heat 1 tablespoon of canola oil in a non-stick fry pan over medium to high heat.

Add 1 teaspoon of sliced red onion, cook until onion is fragrant and slightly golden.

Add a few slices of pork belly and prawns, make sure that the pork and prawns are cooked through.

Pour a thin layer of pancake batter into the pan and swirl the pan to spread the batter.

Add a handful of mung bean sprouts and then cover the pan with a lid.

Cook for 2-3 minutes, then remove the lid and cook for a further 3-4 minutes to ensure the batter is completely cooked and has a golden crispy edge.

Fold the pancake in half and set aside. Repeat this cooking process with the remaining pancake ingredients.

To serve, place all freshly washed green leaves on a big platter and the pancakes on a separate platter.

To eat, break a piece of the pancake onto a lettuce leaf, add a few leaves of each of the herbs, then roll it up and dip in the dipping sauce.

969 Matakana Road
Matakana 0985

021 061 4100
Phuong@vietqfoods.co.nz
www.vietqfoods.co.nz

BEETROOT BURGER

My wife and I don't eat any meat but we do enjoy a nice veggie burger. These beetroot burgers are healthy and delicious, and they fill you up.

Christian Thomas

SERVES: 6-12 | PREP: 15 MINS + CHILLING | COOK: 1 ½ HOURS | DIFFICULTY: EASY

3 large beetroots (about 450g), skin on, trimmed

½ cup brown rice, uncooked

1 tsp extra virgin olive oil

1 medium brown onion, diced

3-4 garlic cloves, minced

2 Tbsp cider vinegar

¼ cup rolled oats

800g (2 cans) black beans

¼ cup prunes, finely chopped

1 Tbsp extra virgin olive oil

2 tsp mustard (Dijon or wholegrain honey)

2-3 tsp smoked paprika, to taste

1 tsp ground cumin

½ tsp ground coriander

½ tsp dried thyme

1 large egg (optional, leave out for vegan burgers)

Salt and pepper

Extra olive oil for cooking

6-12 burger buns

Preheat oven to 200°C.

Wrap the beetroots loosely in foil and roast until tender (50-60 minutes). Set aside to cool.

Meanwhile, cook the rice until a little over-cooked. Drain and set aside to cool.

While the rice is cooking, heat a teaspoon of olive oil in a pan over medium-high heat. Add the onions and a pinch of salt. Stir the onions and cook until they are golden (10-12 minutes). Add the garlic and cook for 30 seconds. Pour in the cider vinegar and reduce. Remove from heat and set aside to cool.

Process the oats until they have reduced to a fine flour.

Drain and rinse one can of beans and blend in a food processor. Scatter the prunes on top. Pulse in 1 second bursts until the beans are roughly chopped (not mushy). Put the mixture into a large mixing bowl. Drain and rinse the second can of beans and add these whole to the mixture.

Scrape the skins off the beetroots and grate. Squeeze out any excess liquid.

Combine the beetroots, cooked rice, sautéed onions, beans, olive oil, mustard, smoked paprika, cumin, coriander and thyme. Add salt and pepper to taste, then add the oatmeal flour and egg (if using) and mix well. Cover and refrigerate for at least 2 hours or overnight.

When ready to cook, take a handful of the patty mixture and shape it into a thick patty the size of your burger buns.

Heat a pan over a high heat and add a few tablespoons of olive oil. Cook the patties for 2 minutes on each side then cover, reduce the heat to medium-low and cook for a further 4 minutes.

Serve on burger buns or lightly toasted sandwich bread with fresh salad.

Notes: The patty mix can be kept in the fridge for up to three days before cooking.

After school care

BRICK BAY CHERMOULA LAMB

Inspired by the bounty of Brick Bay, we love the contrast of the tender lamb, the sweetness of the fresh figs, the creaminess of the yoghurt and feta and the crunch of the seeds.

From the Glass House Kitchen at Brick Bay

SERVES: 4 | PREP: 30 MINS + CHILLING | COOK: 20 MINS | DIFFICULTY: EASY

600g lamb fillet or backstrap
60g Chermoula paste
½ butternut pumpkin, peeled, deseeded
3 garlic cloves, finely chopped
Rosemary twig, finely chopped
¼ tsp ground nutmeg
½ tsp ground cinnamon
Salt and pepper
Olive oil
1 baby cos lettuce
6 ripe figs, stems removed, quartered
150g Puhoi Valley goat's milk feta, crumbled
Fresh herbs (mint, coriander, basil), chopped
Toasted sunflower seeds
Balsamic vinegar
125g Greek yoghurt
Chutney

CHERMOULA PASTE:
1 cup fresh coriander, roughly chopped
¼ cup fresh parsley, roughly chopped
4 garlic cloves, chopped
1 Tbsp minced ginger
2 Tbsp white vinegar
1 lemon, zested & juiced
1 Tbsp ground paprika
1 Tbsp ground cumin
1 red chilli, deseeded
2 Tbsp olive oil

Combine all chermoula paste ingredients in a food processor. Marinate lamb (for backstrap, remove fat if preferred) in chermoula paste, season with salt and pepper, cover and refrigerate for a minimum of 4 hours or overnight.

Preheat oven to 220°C. Roughly cut butternut into medium sized wedges. Combine garlic, rosemary, nutmeg, cinnamon, salt, pepper and 1 tablespoon of olive oil and toss through the butternut.

Roast on a baking tray lined with baking paper for approximately 12 minutes until tender.

Preheat BBQ or grill until hot. While grill is heating, remove lamb from the fridge to bring the temperature up. BBQ the lamb to your preferred doneness - we prefer medium rare. Rest for 5 minutes prior to slicing. Cut the lamb into large slices.

Rinse and separate cos lettuce leaves. We use the inside leaves as they are crunchy and smaller.

To serve, place the cos leaves, figs, butternut, sliced lamb and crumbled goats cheese onto a large platter. Garnish with fresh herbs, sunflower seeds, olive oil, balsamic vinegar and season to taste. Add dollops of chutney and yoghurt on the plate. Perfect served with Brick Bay Rosé.

Notes: Chutney to serve (we use a caramelised red onion, beetroot & pear). Store any remaining paste in an airtight container in the fridge for 1 week.

Brick Bay
MATAKANA
Rosé
2017

Brick Bay is a loved landscape, filled with ideals, inspirational art, food and wine.
The Glass House is the spectacular home of Brick Bay Wines where our chefs create contemporary NZ cuisine, inspired by our farm produce, orchards, gardens and local ingredients. We showcase contemporary sculpture featuring some of the most exciting artists working in NZ today.
The 2km sculpture trail meanders past lakes, vineyard, forest and open pasture, and offers unexpected intimate views alongside stunning panoramas.
Open daily,
10am - 5pm
17 Arabella Lane,
Snells Beach
www.brickbay.co.nz
Brick Bay
Est. 1986

Dining together is one of life's great pleasures and what better way to meet your neighbours than at the Point Wells Connoisseurs Club.

For over 35 years locals have gathered on the third Thursday of every month to swap stories, have a laugh and share a 'pot luck' meal.

'This is an old-fashioned village, where everyone knows everyone, and there's always someone available to help when you need it,' says longtime connoisseur Noeline Cranston.

There's no need to get fancy - the focus is on nourishing, satisfying fare, designed to be shared. Bring along a dish, a beverage, a gold coin donation and pull up a chair at the Point Wells village table.

This chapter is brought to you by

Plume

Main Meals

The Connoisseurs Club, Point Wells

COMMUNITY EVENTS
THE FITNESS LEAGUE
10am Monday
CROQUET CLUB
LIBRARY
Monday 7 - 8 pm
Wednesday
Friday 3: -5pm
GARDEN CLUB
4th Thursday of each month 1:30pm
BOWLING CLUB
4 Kowhai Road

POINT WELLS
EST.
1948
GENERAL STORE

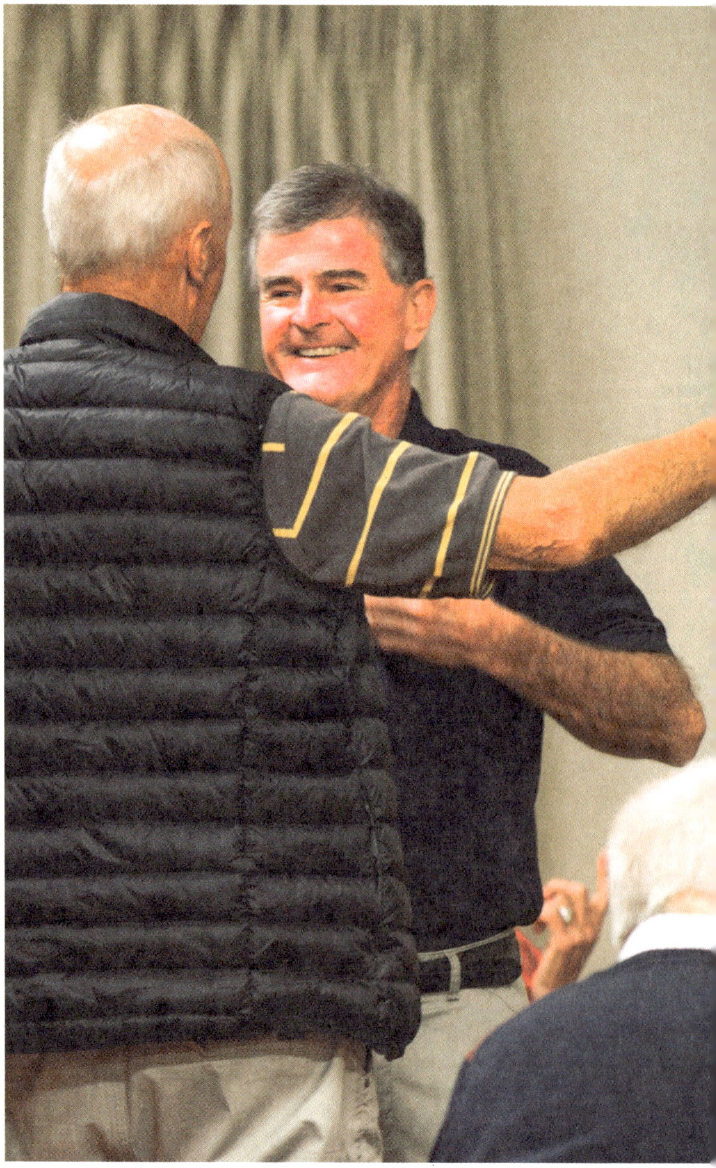

ROLLED BBQ PORK BELLY

This is a great recipe that can be made several days in advance. It always goes down a treat with the whole family. It's a winner.

Owain Meredith

SERVES: 6 | PREP: 15 MINS | COOK: 2 HOURS | DIFFICULTY: MEDIUM

2kg boneless pork belly

3 tsp smoked paprika

½ cup fresh oregano

3 tsp garlic, chopped

4-5 dried apricots, chopped (optional)

Zest and juice of 1 lemon

Salt and pepper

1 cup apple juice

1 cup chicken stock

Bay leaves

Oil for cooking

Preheat oven to 150°C.

Remove the skin from the pork belly and butterfly the pork belly by cutting through the middle to the far edge but not right through. You should now have a piece of pork twice the size and half the thickness.

Rub the pork with smoked paprika and cover evenly with the oregano, garlic, apricots, lemon zest, salt and pepper. Splash lemon juice over the pork.

Roll the belly up tightly and tie with string.

Season the rolled pork and sear in a large pan with oil until golden.

Remove from the pan and place in a snug fitting oven dish.

Cover with apple juice, chicken stock and bay leaves, then cover with foil and cook for 2 hours until tender.

Cool in the juice then remove and refrigerate until required.

Remove string and cut into 2cm round slices. Brush with oil, salt and pepper and cook until golden on a BBQ, chargrill or in a frying pan.

Serve immediately with a salad of your choice.

INDIVIDUAL VEGETARIAN MOUSSAKA

This dish evokes memories of our travels around Greece and Turkey and is a family favourite.

Chris Casarelia

SERVES: 2 | PREP: 30 MINS | COOK: 30-40 MINS | DIFFICULTY: MEDIUM

50g green or Puy lentils

100ml water

1 eggplant (75g), chopped into small cubes

Salt

4 Tbsp olive oil

2 small onions, finely chopped

100g green capsicum, finely chopped

2 garlic cloves, crushed

4 Tbsp red wine or dry cider

2 Tbsp tomato puree

Pinch of ground cinnamon

2 tsp parsley, chopped

Salt and freshly ground black pepper

TOPPING:

2 large eggs

4 Tbsp natural yoghurt

2 Tbsp parmesan cheese, grated

Nutmeg, freshly grated

Preheat oven to 180°C.

Cook the lentils in 100ml of water (no salt added) at a gentle simmer for about 30 minutes or until they are softened and all the water has been absorbed.

Place the eggplant cubes in a colander, sprinkle them with a little salt and olive oil and leave to rest for 10-15 minutes. This helps take the bitterness out and soften them. Then wash off the salt and squeeze them dry in a clean tea towel.

Heat 2 tablespoons of oil in a pan and cook the onions and capsicums together until they are softened (8-10 minutes). Remove and place on a plate.

Add the remaining oil to the pan and cook the eggplant, which will take about 10 minutes to soften. Add the garlic, cook for 1 minute then return the onion and capsicum to the pan.

Mix the wine and tomato purée together with the cinnamon and parsley in a jug, then pour this into the vegetable mixture.

Stir in the softened lentils, season with salt and pepper, then mix until everything is thoroughly combined.

Spoon the mixture into two, 13cm ramekins.

To make the topping, beat the egg together with the yoghurt, parmesan and a little freshly grated nutmeg and pour this over the top of the vegetables.

Bake in the oven for 30 minutes or until the top is puffy and golden.

Serve with brown rice or wholewheat pita bread.

The annual kids versus adults soccer game, Point Wells

The historic Big Omaha Wharf on Whangateau Estuary

Hamish Blampied, Phil Holt & Duncan Anderson

SMOKIN' HOT

After becoming part owner of The Matakana pub in 2012, Duncan Anderson got serious about barbecued meats. 'I wanted to create unique dishes for the pub, like slow-cooked ribs and brisket.'

When his sister relocated from the US to New Zealand, Duncan casually asked if he could slip 'a barbecue' into her container. Said barbecue was a 1-tonne steel offset grill shaped like a locomotive, with fire at one end of the barrel and meat at the other. 'Indirect cooking is about having the heat and the meat on opposite sides.'

Smokey aromas were soon wafting from the pub's garden, catching the attention of fellow rib aficionado, Phil 'he brings the party' Holt. The pair began sharing beers and comparing flavours. 'It's a bit like winemaking', says Duncan. 'We blend our own rubs and glazes, tasting as we go until we get it right.

'Cooking becomes part of the event'

In 2016, the pair formed the Matakana Smoke Eaters with Hamish Blampied and Rochelle 'Rocky' Hicks, entering New Zealand's first major barbecue competition, Meatstock. They camped overnight at the Auckland showgrounds, waking periodically to glaze the meat, and taking second prize for lamb.

As for the secret to perfect ribs? 'Ask your butcher for ribs with some meat on them,' says Duncan. 'In New Zealand, we often sacrifice the ribs for pork belly. '

Wood influences the flavour, and Duncan recommends windfall puriri, pohutukawa or pear.

Duncan has now moved on from the pub but still enjoys lighting up the barbecue with friends. 'It's a convivial thing. Cooking becomes part of the event.'

Light the fire, pour a drink and enjoy.

BBQ SPARE RIBS

Ribs are best cooked long and slow, until the meat falls into your fingers. Enjoy with friends and a light summer lager, or pale ale.

Duncan Anderson

SERVES: 6 -8 | PREP: 30 MINS | COOK: 3 ½ HOURS | DIFFICULTY: EASY

- 2-3 rib racks
- ⅓ cup ground black pepper
- ¼ cup sea salt
- 1 heaped Tbsp smoked paprika
- 1 Tbsp onion powder or granulated onion
- 1 tsp garlic powder or granulated garlic
- 1 tsp mustard powder
- 1 tsp celery salt
- Dash of chilli powder or cayenne for spice if your kids can handle it
- 1 cup brown sugar
- BBQ sauce
- Butter
- Apple juice

Trim unwanted fat from the ribs and pull off the silver skin, this allows more flavour from the dry rub spices to penetrate the meat.

To make the rib dust, whisk the dry ingredients together, breaking up the chunks to get an even mixture. Sprinkle liberally over the ribs and leave for an hour (covered) before cooking.

In a Weber Kettle, light the charcoal or briquettes and push to one side for indirect cooking. Wait for the embers to establish (approx 15 minutes). If using a gas BBQ, use one or two burners at one end. Put the ribs on the kettle/BBQ at the opposite end of the heat source. Cook for 2 hours at around 120°C until mahogany brown.

Pull ribs off and dab on some BBQ sauce, butter and a dash of apple juice and wrap tightly in foil. Put them back on the BBQ and cook for another hour until ribs are tender and moist. Then unwrap them from the foil, dab with more BBQ sauce, sprinkle on more rib dust and finish in the BBQ for another 20-30 minutes to set the sauce. Take off and carve on a large board, cutting on the same angle as the ribs.

Notes: Ribs are best cooked indirectly using charcoal in a Weber Kettle or similar solid fuel BBQ. You can use a gas BBQ but keep the ribs away from the flames and use a low heat. Putting together an explosively flavoured seasoning mix is not only fun, it's cheaper than buying it pre-made.

Plume

CHICKEN & FEIJOA CURRY

This is our go-to meal when the feijoas on our trees are going for gold! It is a mild light curry that is sweet rather than spicy.

The Smith Family

SERVES: 4 | PREP: 20 MINS | COOK: 30 MINS | DIFFICULTY: EASY

¼ cup olive oil

4 chicken breasts, skinned, boned, cut into bite-size pieces

1 onion, peeled, thinly sliced

2 carrots, peeled, thinly sliced

2 red, yellow or green capsicums, diced

1 garlic clove, peeled, crushed

5 ripe feijoas, peeled, halved lengthways, cut into thick slices

1 Tbsp curry powder

½ tsp salt

¼ tsp allspice

⅛ tsp ground black pepper

1 litre chicken stock

1 Tbsp cornflour, mixed with 2 Tbsp cold water

In a heavy based frying pan, heat a little olive oil.

Sauté the chicken for 3 minutes until just starting to brown, remove from the pan.

Heat remaining oil and sauté onion, carrots, capsicums and garlic for 5 minutes.

Add chicken back to the pan with feijoas, curry powder, salt, allspice and pepper.

Heat chicken stock in a separate pot until simmering and then add to the chicken and vegetable mixture.

Bring to the boil, then reduce heat to a simmer.

Add cornflour mix to thicken.

Cover and simmer for 20 minutes.

Serve with basmati rice.

Notes: The curry can be accompanied with minted yoghurt and/or mango chutney and naan bread. This is a watery curry so we often add a can of drained chickpeas and a cup of peas at the simmering stage to thicken. The curry can be frozen.

GREEN TEQUILA ROASTED CHICKEN

This simple chicken dish, which we enjoyed at a local restaurant one evening in Oaxaca, Mexico, has become a favourite in our family. Serve it with a sliced tomato and avocado salad and some freshly made warm tortillas to mop up the juices.

Lynn Slovak

SERVES: 4 | PREP: 15 MINS | COOK: 1 HOUR | DIFFICULTY: MEDIUM

Large bunch fresh coriander

Smaller bunch fresh mint

Juice and zest of 2 limes

1 fresh green chili, deseeded

1 Tbsp honey

3 large garlic cloves, peeled

1 tsp sea salt

½ medium white onion, roughly chopped

2 Tbsp tequila blanco

3 Tbsp good quality olive oil

1 whole chicken, approx 1.5kg, cleaned, backbone removed (spatchcocked)

Place all ingredients except the chicken in a food processor on high and blitz until you have a thick paste, adding a little more oil if necessary.

Lay the chicken out on a board and wearing disposable gloves to protect you from the heat of the chilli, rub the paste all over both sides of the chicken and under the skin where you can reach.

Place the chicken into a large resealable plastic bag to marinate in the fridge for several hours.

Preheat the oven to 200°C.

Remove the chicken from the bag and arrange it, skin side up, in a shallow roasting dish.

Pour any remaining marinade over the top, cover loosely with a sheet of foil and cook for 30 minutes.

Remove the foil, spoon some of the juices over the top of the chicken and continue to cook for a further 30 minutes, or until the thigh juices run clear when pierced with the point of a small sharp knife.

Allow to rest for 10 minutes before serving.

Michael Bernard

MIKE THE KNIFE

It was 'serendipity' that led Michael Bernard to sharpen knives at the Matakana Village Farmers' Market.

Every Saturday morning he sets up his tools and grinders, chatting happily to restauranteurs and keen home cooks as he casts a careful eye over the state of their blades. He can tell if you've put them through the dishwasher (a big no-no), or left it too long between sharpenings. 'I was a chef, so these are my trade tools,' says Michael.

'It's an incredibly positive, honest job'

Back in 2011, the Snells Beach resident had just been made redundant from his month-on month-off job as cook on a tugboat, when he heard the knife sharpening business was up for sale. After more than three decades in the kitchen, including running his own pizzeria and seven years in ships' galleys, he was more than ready to step out into the daylight.

He quickly came to love the market and the satisfaction of a task well done. 'It's an incredibly positive, honest job,' says Michael. 'You take a blunt knife, make it sharp and the customer walks away happy. They know immediately if you've done a good job.'

Word of Michael's sharpening skills soon spread. He now travels around Auckland, sharpening knives in fine establishments such as Soul Bar, Baduzzi and The Hunting Lodge as well as local eateries like Ascension Wine Estate and Sawmill Brewery. 'I don't want to be a chef anymore, but I love seeing what they're doing with new ingredients, techniques and styles.'

Plume

Michael's Top Tips for Knife Care

- A decent 180-200mm chef-style knife and a 75-90mm vegetable knife are enough for most situations – the rest are just handy additions.
- Always store your knives in a block, on a magnet or in a sleeve – the edge will get damaged bumping around in a drawer.
- Never put your knives in the dishwasher - the pressure of the water will damage the handle and blunt your knife. Always wash knives by hand.
- Choose wooden chopping boards over plastic or glass - the first cut on a glass board can take the edge off a good knife.
- Never use a knife edge to scrape chopped food off a cutting board – instead, flip the knife over and use the back of the blade for scraping.
- Professionally sharpened knives will stay sharp for 4-6 months. A regular, gentle stroke on butcher's steel at a 20-degree angle will keep them sharp even longer.

DRINKS MENU

CHORIZO, CHICKEN & TOMATO ESTOFADOS

This Spanish style hot pot is so full of flavour and yet so simple to make. It is one of those great dishes that can be prepared the day before and it is just as delicious if you use pork or lamb.

From the Kitchen of The Matakana Pub

SERVES: 4 | PREP: 15 MINS | COOK: 35 MINS | DIFFICULTY: EASY

8 corn fed chicken thighs (preferably free range)

Rice bran oil

1 tsp smoked paprika

Salt and pepper

¼ cup chorizo, diced

¼ cup red onion, diced

¼ cup carrot, diced

1 tsp smoked paprika

2 sticks celery, diced

2 garlic cloves, chopped

1 bay leaf

6-10 saffron threads

1 tsp fresh oregano

250ml chicken stock

1 can cannellini beans, drained, rinsed

1 can crushed tomatoes

100g baby spinach

Preheat a large heavy based pot, big enough to fit all of the ingredients.

Rub the chicken with a little oil, the paprika and season with salt and pepper.

Place the oil, chicken and chorizo in the pan and sauté for 2-3 minutes until the chicken begins to colour. Remove the thighs and set to one side.

Add the onion, carrot, smoked paprika, celery, garlic, bay leaf, saffron and oregano. Continue to sauté for a further 1-2 minutes until all the vegetables are tender.

Add the stock, beans, tomatoes and chicken thighs and simmer gently for 30 minutes or until the chicken is cooked through. Season to taste.

Stir through the spinach, divide the ingredients into four bowls and serve with grilled polenta and crusty bread.

Michelle Moir (1969–2017)

THE MAGIC OF THE MOMENTS IN BETWEEN

Peek into the living rooms of many a Matakana home, and you'll find striking black and white family portraits. Images of children lost in the moment, caught mid-twirl, suspended from a tree or firing a mischievous look at a sibling.

For documentary photographer Michelle Moir, this was 'the magic of the moments in between'. Forget awkward family poses and forced smiles; in her emotive images Michelle intuitively captured the essence of her subjects and their family bonds.

After growing up on a dairy farm in the Whangaripo Valley, Michelle explored her gift for photography at the Elam School of Fine Arts, travelling the length of New Zealand capturing first, country women, and later Maori women, in their home surroundings. Her work received critical acclaim; Images of Maori Women – Mataahua Wāhine toured New Zealand as a major exhibition and both collections were published by Tandem Press.

In 2011, Michelle, her husband Gavin and daughter Loula returned to Matakana, buying a tiny rundown farmhouse with an overgrown orchard on nine acres of land. Within weeks she had 'Michelle-ified' the long neglected garden, with a truckload of white pebbles and an Italianate outdoor table fit for the silverware, crystal and abundance of blooms she famously lavished on every special celebration.

Michelle was known for her generous platters, often produced at a moment's notice laden with olives, cheeses and cured meats from the Farmers' Market. There was always a special flourish – a sprig of rosemary tied in twine alongside a dish of guava jelly made to her grandmother's handwritten recipe.

In 2016, shortly after work was completed on their dream home on the hill above the old farmhouse, Michelle was diagnosed with cancer. Before she passed away, she took time to share the recipe for one of her favourite family meals with the Matakana community she loved so dearly.

Plume

MEDITERRANEAN EGGPLANT BAKE

This has always been a staple vegetarian meal in our family and it's always enjoyed by meat eaters too.

Michelle Moir

SERVES: 6 | PREP: 30 MINS | COOK: 45 MINS | DIFFICULTY: EASY

1 large eggplant (approx 750g)

1 egg

1 Tbsp water

½ cup dry breadcrumbs or 1 cup gluten free rolled oats, finely processed

Oil for cooking

1 medium onion

8 large tomatoes (or 2 tins tomatoes)

1 garlic clove, crushed

Juice of 1 lemon

Fresh basil (or 1 tsp dried basil)

1 tsp mixed spice

¼ tsp cinnamon

1 Tbsp sugar

½ cup water

½ tsp salt

Freshly ground pepper

1 cup cheese or goat feta, grated

Preheat oven to 180°C.

Cut the eggplant into slices about 1cm thick. In a shallow dish big enough to hold the slices, beat the egg with the water, just enough to combine. Dip the eggplant slices first in the egg, then in the crumbs, coating both sides. Fry slices in oil until brown on both sides. Leave to drain on paper towels.

In another pan, sauté the sliced onions in 1 tablespoon of oil until lightly browned. Add the tomatoes, garlic, lemon juice, basil, mixed spice, cinnamon, sugar, water, salt and pepper, and simmer until the onion is tender.

Lightly grease a shallow casserole dish (about 23cm × 30cm), then put half the browned eggplant slices into the dish, cutting them to fit if necessary. Pour half the tomato mixture over this layer, top with remaining eggplant, then the remaining tomato mixture. Top with cheese.

Bake uncovered for 45 minutes, or until the top browns and the eggplant is very tender. Do not hurry the cooking. Leave to stand for at least 10 minutes before serving.

Looking across Whangateau Estuary to Ti Point

CROATIAN STUFFED PEPPERS

(PUNJENE PAPRIKE)

This traditional dish is very popular in Croatia and in Croatian homes here in NZ. In the middle of the intense heat of summer you'll find people eating this as well as hot chicken or beef soup! It's my absolute favourite.

Helena Ujdur

SERVES: 6 | PREP: 50 MINS | COOK: 1 HOUR | DIFFICULTY: EASY

8-10 green peppers (capsicums)

30g lard or olive oil

10g onions, minced

250g minced beef

250g minced pork

50g rice

1 egg

Salt and pepper

SAUCE:

40g lard or butter

40g plain flour

500g tomato juice

Salt

20g sugar

100g sour cream

Wash the green peppers and carefully remove the core and seeds, leaving the empty pepper intact.

Sauté finely minced onion in lard/oil. When transparent remove from the heat and add minced beef and pork.

Parboil the rice until half cooked and add to the meat.

Add 1 whole egg, salt and pepper. Mix well into a compact stuffing.

Stuff each pepper with stuffing until full.

In a pot, melt lard/butter and sauté flour until brownish.

Add tomato juice, salt and sugar. Add water if needed.

Roast each pepper in a frying pan in some oil, making sure they don't overcook or burn.

Put the peppers into the pot with the sauce and cook for 1 hour.

Add sour cream at the end when serving.

MIDDLE EASTERN LAMB SHANKS

This dish is an easy one-pot wonder that combines beautiful Kiwi lamb with our Middle Eastern heritage and takes Mum back to her childhood memories of sidewalk rotisserie chickens, syrupy Luqmat al Qadi (Arabic yeast donuts) and dried apricot paste wrapped in yellow cellophane.

The Beadsmoore Family

SERVES: 4 | PREP: 15-20 MINS | COOK: 2 HOURS | DIFFICULTY: EASY

4 large lamb shanks

2 large red onions, chopped

½ cup olive oil

3 large garlic cloves, peeled, chopped

1½ tsp baharat (Middle Eastern spice mixture)

1 tsp ground turmeric

800g tin chopped tomatoes

1 cup water

2 Tbsp (heaped) tomato paste

2 fresh bay leaves

1 lemon, grated rind and juice

¼ of a preserved lemon, thinly sliced rind only

1-2 Tbsp pomegranate molasses

GARNISH:

½ cup pomegranate seeds

Sumac to sprinkle

Preheat oven to 190°C.

Rinse the lamb shanks under cold running water, pat dry with a cotton cloth and put to one side.

In a heavy ovenproof dish, fry the chopped onions on a low heat with the olive oil until soft but not browned.

Add the garlic, baharat and turmeric and continue to gently fry for another minute.

Add all of the remaining ingredients (except those for the garnish) and bring to a gentle boil.

Turn the heat down and simmer the sauce for about 5 minutes.

Place the lamb shanks into the dish with the sauce. Gently turn and coat the lamb shanks completely with the sauce.

Cover with a lid or aluminium foil and place in the oven for approximately 2 hours, until the meat begins to fall away from the bone.

Plate the shanks on a bed of white rice and pour over the sauce. Sprinkle on some pomegranate seeds and dust rice with a little sumac.

Serve with Arabic bread (khubz) or pita bread.

Notes: Baharat is a mixed spice used in the Gulf and Iraq – it is available in many stores stocking spices but you can make your own.

Mix the following: 1 tsp black pepper powder, ¾ tsp ground coriander, ¾ tsp ground cinnamon, ¾ tsp ground cloves, ¾ tsp ground cumin, 6 tsp ground cardamom, ¾ tsp ground nutmeg, 1½ tsp paprika powder (mild), ¾ tsp ground dried limes and ¾ tsp curry powder (mild).

You can even plan ahead and make your own preserved lemons.

Early morning sun at Point Wells

Shouri Khosravi

VITAL ENERGY

When she arrived in New Zealand from Iran in 2011, Shouri Khosravi fell in love with the country. Sadly, her body did not feel the same way.

Shouri suffered an array of health problems, including asthma, allergies and liver dysfunction, so she decided to try going vegetarian. At the time, she had no intention of adopting what she considered an 'extreme' lifestyle. 'I followed my instinct, listened to my body and eventually ended up raw vegan.'

The transformation was dramatic. 'I'm like a teenager, wondering how to spend all my energy,' laughs Shouri. 'I'm always bouncing and dancing, and I just feel so grateful.'

'I firmly believe this is the way everyone needs to go sooner or later. It's sustainable and very good for our bodies and the environment.'

After settling in 'beautiful, peaceful' Snells Beach, Shouri found herself driving to Auckland each week for organic food supplies.

'I followed my instinct, listened to my body and eventually ended up raw vegan'

And that's how the Hungry Elephant café and organic store came about. 'We serve real food, free from chemicals, MSG, and pesticides,' says Shouri. 'Our hummus doesn't start in a can; we soak and sprout, and make everything possible from scratch.'

While 95 per cent of her diet is raw, Shouri, who comes from a long line of 'very special cooks', still loves the aroma of good food like Adas Polo, a satisfying lentil and rice dish from Iran.

Plume

ADAS POLO

Adas Polo is a traditional Persian dish, made from lentils and rice, and flavoured with turmeric, cardamom and coriander. It looks beautiful, tastes great and offers a complete source of protein for vegans and vegetarians.

Shouri Khosravi

SERVES: 5 | PREP: 20 MINS + SOAKING | COOK: 75 MINS | DIFFICULTY: EASY

½ tsp saffron

½ cup green lentils, soaked for at least 4 hours

¾ cup boiling water

1½ cups basmati rice

1 Tbsp coconut oil

1 tsp salt

3 cups water

1 large brown onion

½ tsp ground turmeric

½ tsp ground coriander

½ tsp ground cinnamon

½ tsp whole caraway seeds

8 whole dates, pitted

½ cup raisins

1 large potato

Oil for frying

Grind saffron with mortar and pestle, add boiling water and set aside to use later.

Place lentils in a medium sized pot, fill with water and bring to the boil. Once boiling, reduce heat and simmer for 15 minutes. Strain and set aside.

Place rice, coconut oil and salt in a separate pot, add 3 cups of water and bring to the boil. Once boiling, reduce heat and simmer until all of the water has been absorbed. Remove from heat and set aside. The rice shouldn't be cooked through at this stage.

While lentils and rice are cooking, finely slice the onion and gently fry until golden brown.

Then add turmeric, coriander, cinnamon and caraway seeds. Fry for another 3 minutes then remove the onions and set aside but keep the oil in the pan.

Using the same pan and oil, combine and gently fry the dates and raisins for 3–5 minutes. Set aside.

Once rice and lentils are cooked, add both to a bowl and combine well.

Slice the potato into slices roughly 3mm thick. Use potato slices to make a single layer in a large non-stick pan and gently fry for 5 minutes.

Add a pinch of salt and the saffron water. Then add the rice and lentils slowly, trying not to disturb the potato layer. Cover with a lid and cook on a low heat for 20 minutes.

To serve, scoop out the rice and lentil mixture slowly. Some of the rice will be yellow from the saffron. Try not to mix the white and yellow rice too much and if you can, layer the rice in a dish with white rice at the bottom and yellow on top for a nice visual effect.

Remove the potatoes from the pan and place on one side of the dish.

Spread onions evenly over the top of the rice then finish it off by garnishing with dates and raisins.

James Graham

PASSION IN THE VINES

According to winemaker James Graham, there is a 'real authenticity' underpinning the Matakana wine scene. 'It's an impassioned group of people putting their heart and soul into what they do.'

James studied viticulture (the science of grapes) and oenology (the science of winemaking) at Lincoln University, before spending the late 90s vintage-hopping between Oregon, South Africa and Europe. 'Every vintage is different, and in every place you discover a new mindset, even if you're doing a simple job. Wine is a shared passion, so passing on information and knowledge is part of the experience.'

James came home in late 1999, taking a job in Marlborough where he met his wife Phuong, who was running a wine laboratory. The pair moved to Matakana in 2004, where James acts as a consultant to a number of boutique vineyards, as well as wineries in West Auckland and Marlborough.

'There is a real authenticity underpinning the Matakana wine scene'

Where major wine regions are often known for a single variety driven by commercial imperatives, James says Matakana vintners have more personal ambitions. 'Some might want a vineyard in a valley or overlooking the sea. Others love wines from the Rhône or Bordeaux.'

'Originally there were a lot of Bordeaux-style reds. Now there are Italian varietals, pinot gris, chardonnay and increasingly, rosé. Others are trying albariño, a hardy grape from the north west of Spain.'

While the production scale is smaller, some things remain the same. 'Matakana vineyards are boutique and hand-picked, but you've still got the same pressures – ripeness, weather, the logistics of picking and making the best wine that you can.'

Plume

Local vintner Clyde Cooper of Runner Duck Estate

TAHINI BAKED MEATBALLS

Our family makes this recipe a lot. The kids love helping with rolling the meatballs, so it's one we can all make together.

The Hughes Family

SERVES: 4-6 | PREP: 20 MINS | COOK: 20 MINS | DIFFICULTY: MEDIUM

TAHINI SAUCE:

150ml tahini paste

150ml water

70ml white wine vinegar

1 garlic clove, crushed

Salt

MEATBALLS:

35g stale white bread, crusts removed

300g minced beef

300g minced lamb

3 garlic cloves, crushed

35g parsley, finely chopped

2½ tsp ground cinnamon

1 egg

Salt and pepper

Olive oil for frying

Parsley, roughly chopped

Lemon zest

Preheat oven to 220°C.

To make the tahini sauce, in a bowl mix the tahini paste, water, vinegar, garlic and a pinch of salt. Whisk well until it turns smooth and creamy, with a thick, sauce-like texture. You might need to add some more water.

Soak the bread in water for 2-3 minutes until it goes soft. Squeeze out most of the water and crumble the bread into a mixing bowl. Add beef, lamb, garlic, parsley, cinnamon, egg, and salt and pepper to taste.

Mix with your hands. Shape the meat mixture into balls, about the size of golf balls.

Pour olive oil into a frying pan and shallow fry your balls, turning as you go, until they are brown on the outside.

Put meatballs on paper towel to soak up the oil then place the meat balls in a single layer in an ovenproof dish. Cook for 5 minutes, then take them out and pour over the tahini sauce and cook for a further 10 minutes. The tahini will take on a touch of colour and thicken up. Meatballs should be just cooked through.

Decorate with the parsley and lemon zest and serve at once.

Plume

AGED BEEF EYE FILLET

Good food, like good wine, takes time to prepare and uses the best ingredients. Relax and cook in a happy frame of mind, then you can sit back and feast thereafter!

From the Kitchen of Plume Restaurant

SERVES: 4 | PREP: 20 MINS | COOK: 30 MINS + 3 HOURS BRAISING | DIFFICULTY: MEDIUM

CONFIT BEEF CHEEKS:

400g beef cheek

2 litres beef stock

500ml Runner Duck Syrah red wine

10g fresh thyme

10g fresh rosemary

1 onion, diced

2 garlic cloves

Salt and pepper to taste

DUCK FAT POTATOES:

500g baby gourmet potatoes

4 Tbsp duck fat

50g fresh parsley, chopped

Salt and pepper to taste

MEDLEY OF VEGETABLES:

100g baby carrots

100g broccolini

100g beans

50ml Runner Duck extra virgin olive oil

HORSERADISH PUREE:

1 small onion, diced

500g peeled parsnip, diced

200ml cream

300ml water

1 tsp vanilla paste

3 Tbsp horseradish paste

180g x 4 Aged Beef Eye Fillet

Preheat oven to 160°C.

To make confit beef cheeks, sear beef cheeks over a high heat, place along with all other ingredients in a baking tray, cover with foil and slow braise for 3 hours. Cool, remove from stock and slice. Reduce the stock in half for the sauce.

To make duck fat potatoes, cut baby potatoes in half, add duck fat and rub well into potatoes.

Increase oven temperature to 180°C and roast the potatoes for 20 minutes (or to your liking) until golden brown.

Add flaky sea salt, pepper and chopped parsley before serving.

To make the medley of vegetables, peel the baby carrots and trim the broccolini and green beans.

Blanch the vegetables in salted boiling water for 3 minutes then toss in a small bowl with flaky sea salt and olive oil.

To make horseradish puree, sauté the onion on low heat, add parsnips and the other ingredients.

Simmer slowly until the parsnip is cooked. Cool and blend to make a puree.

To cook the beef eye fillet, season with salt and pepper, sear on high heat and cook in the oven for 5 minutes at 250°C for medium rare. Rest the eye fillet for 2 minutes before serving.

To plate up, slice beef cheeks in 3 thin slices and pan fry in olive oil. Start with the puree and using a tablespoon, make a tick mark on the left side of the plate.

Place the beef cheeks in the centre and the potatoes beside it. Place the beef eye fillet on top of the potatoes and the medley of vegetables around it.

Pour the reduced beef stock over the eye fillet and serve.

Plume Restaurant, you have it all ...
Great views, ambience, superb food made from scratch, hand tended wines from our vineyard and wine tasting.
An entire vineyard experience!
Plume
The Vineyard Restaurant
49a Sharp Road,
Matakana
09 422 7915
Visit our cellar door at:
www.plumerestaurant.co.nz
Plume

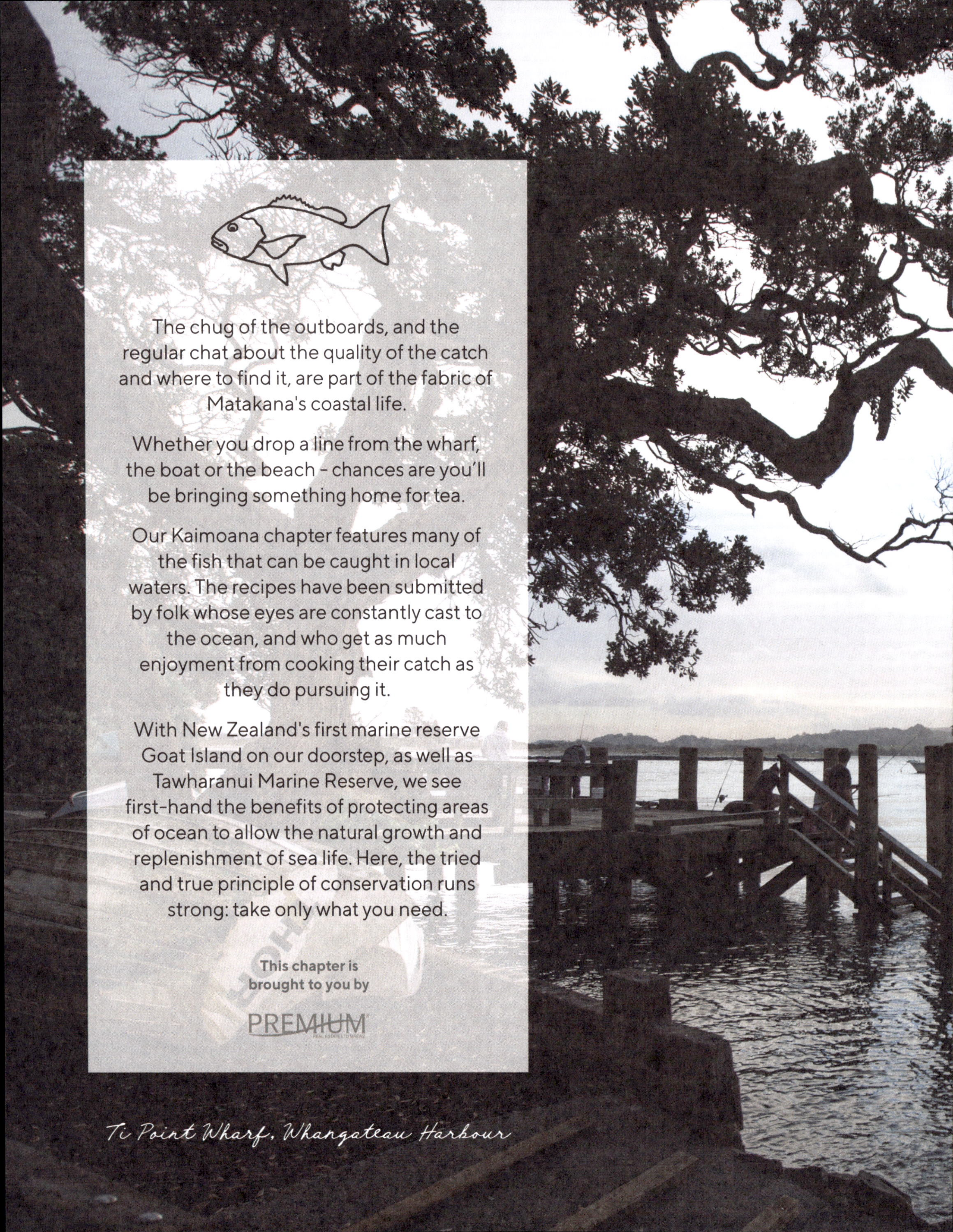

The chug of the outboards, and the regular chat about the quality of the catch and where to find it, are part of the fabric of Matakana's coastal life.

Whether you drop a line from the wharf, the boat or the beach – chances are you'll be bringing something home for tea.

Our Kaimoana chapter features many of the fish that can be caught in local waters. The recipes have been submitted by folk whose eyes are constantly cast to the ocean, and who get as much enjoyment from cooking their catch as they do pursuing it.

With New Zealand's first marine reserve Goat Island on our doorstep, as well as Tawharanui Marine Reserve, we see first-hand the benefits of protecting areas of ocean to allow the natural growth and replenishment of sea life. Here, the tried and true principle of conservation runs strong: take only what you need.

This chapter is brought to you by

PREMIUM

Ti Point Wharf, Whangateau Harbour

Kaimoana

GAMBLER

MATAKANA
OYSTERS
Oysters for the People!
USE

Ti Point Rd
Wharf
Reptile Park

FISH TACOS

We used to make these at the Matakana Village Farmers' Market every Saturday morning, now we make them around the fire when we catch some fresh fish in Kawau Bay. The great thing about tacos is you can make them for 2 or 20 in no time. Tacos are a delicious healthy 10-minute meal.

The O'Sullivan Family

SERVES: 5 | PREP: 15 MINS | COOK: 15 MINS | DIFFICULTY: EASY

600g gurnard (or other white fish)

Olive oil

Sea salt and black pepper

SALSA:

¼ medium red onion

2 large tomatoes

2 or 3 medium to large capsicums (any colour but at least one red)

½ tsp sugar

1 tsp red wine vinegar

½ tsp fish sauce

Salt and ground black pepper

COLESLAW:

¼ small white cabbage

¼ small red cabbage

2 carrots

Tortillas

Aioli

1 small bunch coriander, washed well (use either a few leaves or a small sprig)

Sliced lemons or limes

Chilli

Season the fish before cooking in olive oil, sea salt and black pepper.

To make the salsa, finely chop the red onion, tomatoes and finely dice the capsicums. Combine together in a bowl.

Mix in sugar, red wine vinegar, fish sauce and season to taste with salt and ground black pepper. Refrigerate until needed.

For the coleslaw, finely dice or shred all ingredients and mix together. Refrigerate until ready to use.

Grill the seasoned fish either on a BBQ or over the fire.

Quickly heat the tortillas on the grill or in a small pan so they are warm but not too crunchy.

Then spread one side with aioli, add a large spoonful of coleslaw, top with some grilled fish, drizzle with salsa and garnish with fresh herbs, a squeeze and slice of lemon or lime and chilli if desired, then devour!

Notes: The salsa is the star of this dish if you have time to prepare it.

There's no need to make your own aioli unless you have a favourite recipe, store bought is fine.

The best chilli to use is fresh cut or if it's out of a bottle, use one that is a medium heat or you lose the flavour of the fish and salsa.

We buy our corn tortillas direct from Tio Pablo – it's a cheat but they are so good to carry in a vacuum pack to the fire side.

Tom Searle

WORLD FAMOUS IN LEIGH

Leigh might have the appearance of being a sleepy village, but by 5:00am the crew at Leigh Fisheries are already hard at work.

Tom Searle has been managing the company's 24-hour operations since 2011. Each day he coordinates an array of specialists, from dedicated fishing crews, to packers, truckies and freight forwarders, to ensure the freshest possible fish reaches the tables of Michelin-starred restaurants in Europe and North America 'just in time'.

'It's not just about what happens in the water or at the factory,' says Tom. 'It's an integrated model and it has to be a slick machine.'

Tom studied marine biology at Otago, where he met his wife Caroline. 'I quickly realised I was not a lab coat. I don't believe in science for science's sake. It has to be applicable to industry, or a problem that needs to be solved.'

It was that philosophy that lead Tom to Leigh Fisheries, a company globally renowned for its top quality chilled seafood.

'We start early, so we can get the catch on the first flight out'

'Our main point of difference is the way we catch the fish,' says Tom. 'Eighty per cent is longline caught inshore, with small boats heading out for just one day. And we start early, so we can get the catch on the first flight out.'

Despite the abundance of fish in his life, Tom still enjoys getting out the rods with children Lucy, Freddie and Emily. With the freshest of fish so often on the menu, the Searle family love to enjoy it sashimi-style.

SNAPPER & TREVALLY SASHIMI

In our family, serving up a plate of 'shimi' is like serving up a bowl of chips - the kids crowd around and get stuck in! I love the flavours and textures of different species, and experimenting with different ways of slicing and dicing, using my special sashimi knife gifted to me by our tuna customer in Japan.

Tom Searle

SERVES: 10-40 AS AN ENTRÉE | PREP: 10-30 MINS | NO COOKING | DIFFICULTY: BASIC

- **500g – 2kg fresh snapper**
- **500g – 2kg fresh trevally**
- **Good quality Japanese soy sauce**
- **Root of fresh ginger**
- **Japanese wasabi paste**
- **Japanese ponzu sauce**
- **One lemon or lime**

Fillet fish and remove skin and bones. Slice fillet into 'saku' blocks (square-sided blocks of flesh) and then carefully slice into thin pieces at an angle against the grain of the muscle fibres.

Pour soy sauce into a ramekin and using a zester, grate some fresh ginger on top to taste. Add a generous squirt of wasabi and stir.

Fill a second ramekin with ponzu sauce and add a small squeeze of fresh lime. Arrange on a platter or chopping board and dig in! It's surprising how much the kids will enjoy it too!

Notes: Ideally the fish should be line-caught and killed using the iki-jime method which enhances flesh quality.

Larger fish are not as sweet and can have a tougher texture.

Japanese ponzu sauce is available at most Asian supermarkets.

CRISPY FISH

WITH CHILLI GLAZE

A favourite to serve to family and friends. Fresh, light, fragrant and simple to prepare. The glaze can be made ahead of time and reheated.

Dianne Allan

SERVES: 4 | PREP: 10 MINS | COOK: 15 MINS | DIFFICULTY: EASY

2-3 Tbsp oil

600g firm white fish fillets

2 Tbsp rice flour

Fresh coriander and mint leaves

CHILLI GLAZE:

3cm knob fresh ginger, grated

1 long red chilli, deseeded and finely chopped

½ cup sugar

125ml white vinegar

1 Tbsp fish sauce

To make the glaze, place the ginger, chilli, sugar, vinegar and fish sauce in a small pot and boil gently until liquid thickens (approximately 5-7 minutes). Remove from heat.

Heat oil in a non-stick pan over a medium-high heat. Dredge fish in flour and fry for 2-3 minutes on each side until just cooked through.

Drain on a paper towel before placing on warm plates. Pour the glaze over the fish and top with roughly chopped coriander and mint. Serve with noodles or rice.

Richard Turner

A DISH TO IMPRESS

Back in the day, when former All Black Richard Turner was a single man, he came up with a unique strategy for meeting eligible women: he would host his own version of 90s dating service, Table for Six.

'I'd host a dinner party, invite three single mates, and ask a female friend to do the same,' smiles Richard. 'I had to provide the food, so I was always on the lookout for easy, straightforward and impressive meals.'

One particular recipe proved such a success, it became Richard's signature dinner party dish. 'Paella has that aesthetic – it looks like you've gone to a lot of effort.'

Nowadays, with Richard long married to wife Victoria and a 'netball dad' to Jessica and Casey, he's most likely to be serving up paella for the neighbours in the family's 'very social' Omaha street. 'Not a week goes by that someone isn't having someone else over,' says Richard.

'Paella ... looks like you've gone to a lot of effort.'

Richard grew up in the Hawke's Bay region as the smallest of four boys, and began playing in the National Provincial Championship whilst still at school. His Samoan mum made sure there was always something simmering on the stove for her hungry pack. 'Food was and still is an absolutely vital part of family life.'

Richard and Victoria looked all around New Zealand before deciding to 'put their stake in the ground' here in 2011. For Richard, who played golf at Omaha for years before setting eyes on the beach, it was all about the family lifestyle.

'I love the water, I love that it's safe for the kids to scoot around and I love the changing dynamic with the ebb and flow of locals and visitors,' says Richard. 'It's just a neat little community.'

RICHARD'S PAELLA

This is my go-to dish for dinner parties and it never fails to impress. It's easy (one pan) and yet creates a great visual impact at serving time. I discovered this recipe years ago and have modified it over time (and many dinners) to what it is now.

The Turner Family

SERVES: 6-8 | PREP: 15-20 MINS | COOK: 45 MINS | DIFFICULTY: EASY

6-8 Tbsp olive oil

1 large pack of chicken nibbles or 4 chicken wings and 4 drumsticks

2 medium onions, chopped

6 garlic cloves, crushed

2 capsicums (either red, yellow or orange), sliced

1½ cups Calasparra rice (or Arborio)

3 cups chicken stock

1 pack cherry tomatoes, chopped into quarters

3 cups white wine (substitute with fish stock if preferred)

1 tsp turmeric

1 tsp smoked paprika

1 tsp chilli powder

4 medium chorizo sausages, chopped

2 fish fillets

500g raw prawns

300g calamari

12 scallops (or as many as you like)

8-10 fresh mussels

1½ cups peas or beans

Heat some of the oil and brown the chicken pieces .

Remove from heat and set aside. Add the remaining oil along with the onions and garlic and cook for 3-4 minutes. Then add the capsicum and cook for a further minute.

Add the rice and stir through the pan mixing it well so all the rice is covered with the oil, stir constantly to avoid the rice sticking to the pan.

After 10 minutes add the stock and continue to stir, then add the tomatoes. Add the wine and the chicken pieces then the spices.

Stir thoroughly and then cover (if using a paella pan, use tin foil).

Leave to simmer for 15 minutes with the occasional stir to ensure the rice doesn't stick. Next add the chorizo, the seafood and the peas/beans.

At this stage you can add more liquid (either wine or stock) as it will reduce prior to serving.

Cover the whole pan again and cook for a further 10 minutes to ensure the mussels have opened, then serve and enjoy!

Notes: Ideally you have invested in a paella pan as it makes for a very good visual presentation on serving.

THAI STYLE CURRY
WITH MUSSELS

This dish reminds us of long summer nights in Sydney. Delicious, light and easy to cook.

The Parker Family

SERVES: 4 | PREP: 15 MINS | COOK: 10 MINS | DIFFICULTY: EASY

- 1 bunch coriander
- 3 garlic cloves
- 2cm piece ginger
- 1 lemongrass stalk
- 4 spring onions
- 1 long red chilli
- 2 Tbsp vegetable oil (you can use coconut oil)
- 400ml coconut milk
- 2 lime leaves
- 55g sugar
- 60ml fish sauce
- 2kg mussels
- Juice of 2 limes

Roughly chop half the coriander stalks including the root with garlic, ginger, white part of the lemongrass, 2 spring onions and chilli, then place in a food processor to form a rough paste.

Heat oil in a large pot over a medium heat. Add the paste and cook for around 3 minutes or until fragrant.

Add coconut milk, lime leaves, sugar and fish sauce. Increase the heat to high and bring to the boil.

Add the mussels, cover with a lid and cook for 5-10 minutes or until the mussels are open (remove any that do not open). Squeeze over lime juice and tear over remaining coriander leaves. Slice the remaining spring onions and scatter over the mussels.

Serve and enjoy.

Notes: If you want to make this meal more substantial, serve with jasmine rice or crusty bread.

Tom Walters

VITAMIN SEA

There's a big green shed just outside Matakana Village that is well known to oyster aficionados. Matakana Oysters' owner Tom Walters is a relaxed kind of guy who's been part of the industry for decades. Originally from the Hokianga, Tom first worked in the Mahurangi Harbour as a 17 year-old and came back to buy his own 11 hectare oyster farm there in 2004.

Tom has a degree in marine biology but says being on the job in all seasons is the best way to learn. His oysters are fat and creamy in winter and spring, but it's all about personal preference. 'The French prefer their oysters lean, translucent and salty, so late summer is good for them,' he says.

'I get a big kick out of witnessing the oyster excitement of the true gourmet. But I love heading out on the barge too. You're so close to nature – we see orca, dolphins and rays, the changing colours of the tides, the sunsets and sunrises… it's all a bit magical.'

Matakana Oysters now shares the green shed with Honey by the Sea. Argentinian beekeeper Andres Villegas can often be spotted around Leigh, tending his hives while wearing his safety gear of sunnies and t-shirt. His raw or creamed manuka or coastal bush honey caramelises beautifully over the saltiness of the oysters in this recipe.

Pop in if you're passing – the offbeat banter from Tom and right-hand man Jenta Griffin is always good for a laugh. Check out the witty one-liners chalked outside, and 'may the foreshore be with you'.

BBQ HONEY OYSTERS

This simple dish tastes of local seas, bees, flowers and trees.
To be enjoyed with fine company, for fun times.

Tom Walters

SERVES: 4 | PREP: 5 MINS | COOK: 5 MINS | DIFFICULTY: EASY

2 dozen half shell oysters
¼ cup honey
Hot sauce
2 lemons
Salt and pepper to season

Make a BBQ with manuka wood and reduce the fire to embers.

Place ½ teaspoon of honey on top of each oyster. Drizzle with hot sauce.

Place oysters (in half shell) on the BBQ and grill for 1 minute. Cover with a lid and allow to cook for a further 1-2 minutes.

Remove from the BBQ and season the oysters with a squeeze of lemon juice, salt and pepper.

Serve immediately.

SASHA'S FISH STEW

This is my husband's go-to dish. It is full of fresh seafood and he often makes this for my birthday and other special occasions. I have allergies so it's perfect for me, as it's dairy and egg free.

Sasha Vyle

SERVES: 6 | PREP: 30 MINS | COOK: 1 HOUR | DIFFICULTY: EASY

1 Tbsp olive oil

1 medium onion, finely chopped

2 sticks celery, finely chopped

1 medium carrot, finely chopped

1 medium chilli, finely chopped (seeds in or out depending on heat tolerance)

3 garlic cloves

1 Tbsp fennel seeds, toasted

2 Tbsp tomato paste

½ cup Pernod (or dry white wine)

2 cans tomatoes

1 litre fish stock

2 bay leaves

Salt and pepper

600g firm white fish (e.g. hapuka or monkfish)

12 large prawns, peeled, deveined

½ cup parsley, chopped

12 mussels (steamed separately in white wine and garlic until shells are opened)

Crusty toasted bread

Over a medium heat, add olive oil to a large pot.

Add onion, celery and carrot and stir to coat.

Add chilli, garlic and toasted fennel seeds and sweat for 5 minutes until soft.

Add tomato paste and fry for a couple of minutes.

Add the Pernod and continue to reduce until thick.

Add tomatoes, stock and bay leaves and simmer for 30 minutes, skimming the top every few minutes.

Remove from heat and strain through a conical sieve. Keep the liquid and discard the rest.

Transfer the liquid to a clean pot and increase heat to a simmer.

Check for seasoning and add salt and pepper to taste.

Add the fish and prawns and cook until cooked through

Remove from heat, add parsley and mussels and serve in a deep bowl with crusty bread on the side.

Notes: A variety of fish and seafood can be used.

Abby, Charlie & Chelsy Hurt

OCEAN'S BOUNTY

On a summery Saturday morning there is nothing the Hurt siblings, Abby, Chelsy and Charlie, love more than a spot of fishing. At the turn of the full tide, they'll jump on their bikes and pedal down to their favourite wharf, tucked beneath a pohutukawa on the banks of the Omaha River. There's no need for adults to help with the knots and hooks; these three are old hands at catching sprats.

For Dad Mark and Mum Natascha, this is the life they dreamed of when they decided to raise their family in Point Wells. 'It's the safest place for kids to have that independence and freedom,' says Natascha.

'You don't need a boat. The estuary provides it all'

Mark grew up holidaying here on the edge of the Whangateau Harbour, gathering crabs and oysters, or fishing for flounder and mullet. The couple now relish being able to share these traditions with their children.

'We want our kids to appreciate where food comes from,' says Natascha. 'You don't need a boat, the estuary provides it all'.

The family eat fresh, gathered seafood as much as possible. 'We take just enough for one meal. Maybe it's oysters today, and tomorrow you go and catch a kahawai,' says Natascha.

Back home with the sprats, Abby's job is to scale and gut the sprats, while Chelsy mixes the batter for the fritters. Charlie washes the fillets, then buries the fish guts in the veggie patch. A twist of lemon and they're ready to eat.

OMAHA BAY SPRAT FRITTERS

Sprat fishing is our favourite way to start the day. We love the lemony salty flavour of these fritters, and Charlie loves to help with the filleting so he can sneak a few tasty bites of raw fish before it goes into the batter.

Abby, Chelsy & Charlie Hurt

SERVES: 6-10 | PREP: 5-10 MINS | COOK: 10 MINS | DIFFICULTY: EASY

1 whole egg

1 egg yolk (reserve the egg white)

1 Tbsp flour

Sea salt and freshly ground pepper

6-10 fresh sprats, filleted and cut into 1cm cubes

In a small bowl whisk the whole egg and the yolk with the flour to a smooth batter. Season with sea salt and black pepper.

Stir in the sprats and refrigerate until ready to cook.

To cook and serve, whisk reserved egg white until nearly stiff, then gently fold into the sprat fritter mix.

Heat the BBQ or a non-stick frying pan to a medium-low heat. Add a little butter, then using a small ladle, divide the fritter batter into 6 portions.

Fry a few fritters at a time, turning when golden, which usually takes a minute or so.

Keep warm once cooked and serve with lemon wedges.

A safe mooring in Omaha River

A high tide hang out – wharf jumping in Point Wells

FOVEAUX STRAIT
OYSTERS

AL BROWN'S SNAPPER TARTARE

You can make a tartare out of practically any species of fish. It's a classic dish that can be made from all the offcuts and scrapings from the fish frames, much like ceviche. There are no real rules when it comes to making a fish tartare. You will need a citrus juice or an acid of some sort, plus seasoning and some sort of oil to give the fish some depth and richness. Then it's up to you.

Al Brown

SERVES: 6 AS AN ENTRÉE | PREP: 30 MINS | NO COOKING | DIFFICULTY: BASIC

400g snapper fillet, diced into small pieces

½ cup radish, diced

¾ cup Granny Smith apple, diced

1 lime, zested, pith removed, diced

1 Tbsp lime juice

2 tsp hot sauce

¾ cup extra virgin olive oil

⅓ cup fresh dill, finely chopped

2 Tbsp apple syrup

Flaky sea salt and freshly ground black pepper

Snapper skin crackling to serve (optional)

Place all the ingredients except the seasoning and crackling into a suitably sized bowl and gently mix through. Taste, then season accordingly.

Refrigerate for 5–10 minutes before serving.

To serve, divide up the tartare between individual plates. Use a round cookie cutter if you want a neat circle of tartare, otherwise just use a spoon for a more rustic style.

Serve with snapper skin crackling (if using) on the side.

MUM'S FISH PIE

Every kiwi kid has a story or a memory that is brought back with the smell of a smoked fish pie. Mine is the smell of Dad smoking the freshly caught fish and Mum's resulting yummy pie.

Jeff Evans

SERVES: 8 | PREP: 20 MINS | COOK: 1½ HOURS | DIFFICULTY: MEDIUM

1 Tbsp olive oil

100g streaky bacon, finely chopped

1 onion, finely chopped

2 celery stalks, finely chopped

3 garlic cloves, finely chopped

3 hard-boiled eggs, chopped

500g smoked fish, shredded

Salt and pepper

SAUCE:

25g butter

25g flour

2½ cups milk

MASH:

250g potatoes, chopped

500g kumara, chopped

25g butter

½ cup cream

¼ cup milk

BREADCRUMBS:

2 cups fresh breadcrumbs

50g butter

Preheat oven to 160°C.

Heat oil in a pan over medium heat. Add the bacon, onion, celery and garlic. Cook until the vegetables soften (about 5 minutes).

Turn the heat down to low and cook for 20 minutes, stirring occasionally. The onion will caramelise and the bacon will crisp up.

Then add the hard-boiled eggs and smoked fish, season with salt and pepper and set aside.

For the white sauce, melt butter in a medium sized pot on a medium heat. Add the flour and stir well to form a roux. Add a little milk if necessary and continue stirring until it has a nice liquid consistency.

Add the remaining milk and whisk to remove any lumps so you have a smooth sauce. Continue to stir and simmer until the sauce thickens a little. Add to the bacon, fish and vegetable mixture.

Meanwhile bring water to the boil in a large pot. Add the potatoes, boil for 10 minutes, then add the kumara and boil for a further 10 minutes.

When both the potatoes and kumara are cooked, drain the water and mash them with the butter, cream and milk and set aside.

Place the breadcrumbs into a roasting pan and dot butter around the pan. Bake the breadcrumbs in the oven for 8-10 minutes or until golden and brown.

Turn the oven up to 180°C.

Spread the white sauce and fish mixture into the bottom of an ovenproof dish. Spoon the mashed potato and kumara on top of the filling and sprinkle over the breadcrumbs.

Bake the pie for 30 minutes when it will be bubbling around the sides and ready to eat.

Mike Sutherland & Kirsty McKay

A PLACE LIKE HOME

Kirsty McKay and Mike Sutherland have a clear vision for the Sawmill Brewery's eatery, the Smoko Room. 'We want it to feel like the hospitality of home,' says Kirsty.

This place was built by, and for, a diverse community of local people. The woolshed-style building was designed by Matakana artist and designer, Mike Petre who also styled the interior with Rachel O'Malley. Local tradies crafted fittings from copper plumbing pipes, while knife sharpener Michael Bernard turned the wooden light shades over the bar.

'We wanted it to feel like the hospitality of home'

Craftsmanship, community and 'keeping it real' are integral aspects of the philosophy at the Sawmill Brewery. Mike and Kirsty are known for their quiet-yet-generous community support, and don't mind whether customers arrive in gumboots or high heels.

The Smoko Room's adventurous menu is devised by renowned chef Will Michell, formerly of Floriditas and La Boca Loca in Wellington, who shares the couple's vision of adventurous sharing plates made from local seasonal produce. Will reckons brewing is similar to cooking - it's about combining flavours to create a little bit of alchemy.

'The food is a huge part of the Smoko Room,' says Kirsty. 'The menu changes according to what's around. Will uses everything he can and I'm always blown away by his respect for meat and fish. He uses the whole animal and focuses on sustainably-caught fish.'

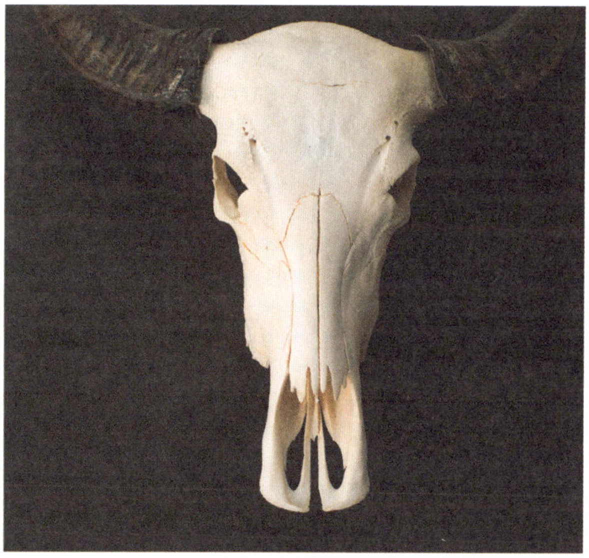

SAWMILL

BAKED FLOUNDER

WITH FENNEL & ROCKET SALAD

The flounder dish is all about using the best produce and letting it shine. The cooking method is simple but really showcases the fish at its best.

From the Kitchen of the Sawmill Brewery and Smoko Room

SERVES: 2 | PREP: 20 MINS | COOK: 15 MINS | DIFFICULTY: BASIC

25ml sherry vinegar

75ml extra virgin olive oil

Salt and pepper

1 fennel bulb

100g rocket

1 whole flounder (300g-450g)

100g tapioca flour

2 Tbsp vegetable oil

100g butter

Preheat oven to 180°C.

To make the dressing, whisk together the vinegar and olive oil with a pinch of salt and pepper.

Finely slice the fennel and toss with the rocket and dressing.

Make a seasoned flour using the tapioca flour and a teaspoon each of salt and pepper.

Place the fish in the seasoned flour to lightly coat, shake off any excess flour.

Using a non-stick pan that can be placed in the oven, heat the pan on the stove and add some vegetable oil.

Once the oil is hot, place the flounder dark skin down in the pan and fry for around 45 seconds until the skin starts to colour.

Flip the flounder over and transfer the pan into the oven for around 7 minutes. Remove the pan from the oven and place back on the stove top and add the butter.

Allow the butter to melt and start to brown then baste the fish for another minute to crisp the skin and add colour.

Serve with salad and enjoy.

OVEN BAKED SALMON

WITH CHILLI & SMOKY TEA

This is my mum's recipe and I love that it's so easy to make. Most of it can be prepared in advance and it can serve a lot of people so it's perfect for when you have a crowd to feed.

The Morris Family

SERVES: 10 | PREP: 5 MINS + REST | COOK: 30 MINS | DIFFICULTY: EASY

¼ cup sugar

2 Tbsp salt flakes

1 Tbsp chilli flakes

1 Tbsp smoky tea

1 salmon side (approx 1kg), skin on

SAUCE:

1 Tbsp cane sugar

1 Tbsp rice vinegar

½ cup Japanese soy sauce

½ Tbsp Asian fish sauce

½ Tbsp ginger, grated

1½ tsp sesame oil

1½ tsp sambal oelek

Mix sugar, salt, chilli and tea.

Rub it onto the salmon on both sides. Put the salmon in a resealable plastic bag and let it sit at room temperature for about 1 hour until the salt/sugar mix has dissolved.

Preheat oven to 150°C.

Cook the salmon in the middle of the oven for about 30 minutes then let it cool.

To make the sauce, mix the sugar and vinegar until the sugar has dissolved. Add the remaining ingredients and refrigerate until ready to serve.

Serve the fish with glass noodles and pour over the sauce.

Notes: Smoky tea can be found in specialty tea shops like T2.

HAPUKA DRY RED CURRY

This is a great example of a curry with no added coconut cream. Using some of New Zealand's freshest fish and accompanied by lots of fresh herbs and lime, this to us is the true taste of Thailand.

From the Kitchen of Smiths

SERVES: 2 | PREP: 15 MINS | COOK: 15 MINS | DIFFICULTY: BASIC

PASTE:

5 large dried red chillies, deseeded, rehydrated

5 fresh red chillies

5 birds eye chillies

4 kaffir lime leaves

4 lemongrass sticks

1 thumb fresh ginger

1 thumb galangal

1 tsp fresh turmeric, grated

2 shallots

4 garlic cloves

BATTER:

3 egg whites

Zest of 2 limes

10ml fish sauce

20ml light soy sauce

300g hapuka fillet

100g rice flour

Palm sugar

Fish sauce

Tamarind

To prepare the red curry paste, roughly chop the chillies, lime leaves, lemongrass, ginger and galangal and place in a food processor with the turmeric, shallots and garlic, and blend to a paste.

To make the batter, whisk the egg whites until they form stiff peaks then lightly fold through the zest, fish sauce and soy sauce. Set aside.

Cut the hapuka into 2cm thick slices, place in flour and dip in the batter. Deep fry until crisp and golden.

Add the paste to a hot pan and season with palm sugar, fish sauce and tamarind. This will add sweet, sour and salt to the dish and the quantity added should be to your personal liking. Once the desired level of seasoning is reached, add the fish to the paste and gently coat.

Serve with your favourite sides; we recommend steamed rice and a whole bunch of fresh mixed herbs.

Notes: You can make the paste a couple of days ahead.

09 422 7360
FB smithsmatakana
IG @smithsmatakana
smiths@stablesmatakana.co.nz
www.stablesmatakana.co.nz/smiths

smiths.
MATAKANA COUNTRY PARK

Smiths is a combination of an old Blacksmiths and a '60s bach. Industrial yet retro. The décor was hand-picked with every piece telling an interesting tale.

In its first 4 months of opening, Smiths is proud to have been awarded the winner of the "Junction Observant Awards 2016" in the Best Restaurants and Bars category.

An impressive wine list showcasing Matakana Wine Country.

Creative cocktails, interesting staff and Matakana's largest sun deck.

Come hang out with friends, graze all afternoon or cosy up in the evening in one of our booths or the heated outdoor area.

Darrel Goosen

TASTE OF AFRICA

Ask Matakana School principal Darrel Goosen about his favourite childhood holidays, and he'll tell you evocative tales of Namibia's 'Skeleton Coast', a 3000 kilometre stretch of foggy Atlantic coastline named for the thousands of shipwrecks that litter its shores.

'My family would drive out there for a few days of surfcasting. Even though storms can be horrendous and the wind can blow you off your feet, we'd put a tent up on the dunes!'

'In all the years I was on the Skeleton Coast, I probably swam three times – it was just too cold. But they were great holidays. My mother was pretty handy at filleting. She'd take the fish we caught and make these amazing fish cakes. They were so yummy on those cold misty days.'

Darrel has adapted the much-loved recipe for the smoked kahawai or snapper available on the Matakana Coast.

'I said to my wife Janet, "I would love to be principal of that school"'

'When I arrived in New Zealand in 1998, I visited Goat Island,' says Darrel. 'As we drove through the "quiet" village of Matakana, I said to my wife Janet, "I would love to be principal of that school"'.

'I had to wait more than twelve years before the opportunity presented itself. I am so glad it did, what a score!'

SKELETON COAST FISH CAKES

Growing up in Namibia, my mother made these fish cakes on our fishing trips along the cold Atlantic Skeleton Coast. Even the black-backed jackals howled when they smelled the delicious aroma wafting over the sand dunes.

Darrel Goosen

SERVES: 6 | PREP: 20 MINS | COOK: 20 MINS | DIFFICULTY: EASY

2 medium sized potatoes

4 smoked fish fillets (kahawai or snapper)

1 egg

1 tsp cornflour

½ tsp salt

Pinch of pepper

Pinch of chilli flakes and/or garlic flakes

Pinch of five spice

½ cup cornflour, extra

Olive oil (not extra virgin)

Peel potatoes, boil until soft and place in a mixing bowl. Flake the fish fillets into the mixing bowl with the potatoes.

Crack the egg into the mixing bowl with the fish and potatoes and add one teaspoon of cornflour.

Add salt, pepper, chilli flakes and/or garlic flakes along with the five spice.

Mash all ingredients together using your hands. When mashed well, roll into balls in the palm of your hand and flatten to approximately 2cm thick.

Spread ½ cup cornflour on a dinner plate and coat the fish cakes lightly in the cornflour.

Heat enough olive oil in a pan to cover half a fish cake. Fry fish cakes for 2 minutes on each side or until golden brown. Drain on a paper towel and serve.

Notes: Make sure you flake your fish finely to avoid bones in your mix. Serve with a dollop of fruit chutney and a slice of lemon.

SCALLOPS & GRAPEFRUIT SALAD

Colourful and very tasty. A great summer dish!

From the Kitchen of Premium Real Estate

SERVES: 2 | PREP: 15 MINS | COOK: 1 MIN | DIFFICULTY: EASY

2 cups baby spinach, washed

1 grapefruit, peeled, sectioned

½ cup pomegranate seeds

1 spring onion, finely sliced

1 Tbsp cooking oil

14 scallops

Olive oil for serving

Mint, chopped (optional)

Chilli, chopped (optional)

In a bowl, mix the baby spinach with the grapefruit, pomegranate and spring onion and set aside.

Heat oil in a fry pan until very hot and cook the scallops for about 30 seconds on each side. They need to remain soft.

Add the scallops to your salad mixture, toss gently then divide between two plates and drizzle with olive oil.

Garnish with the mint and chilli if you are using it.

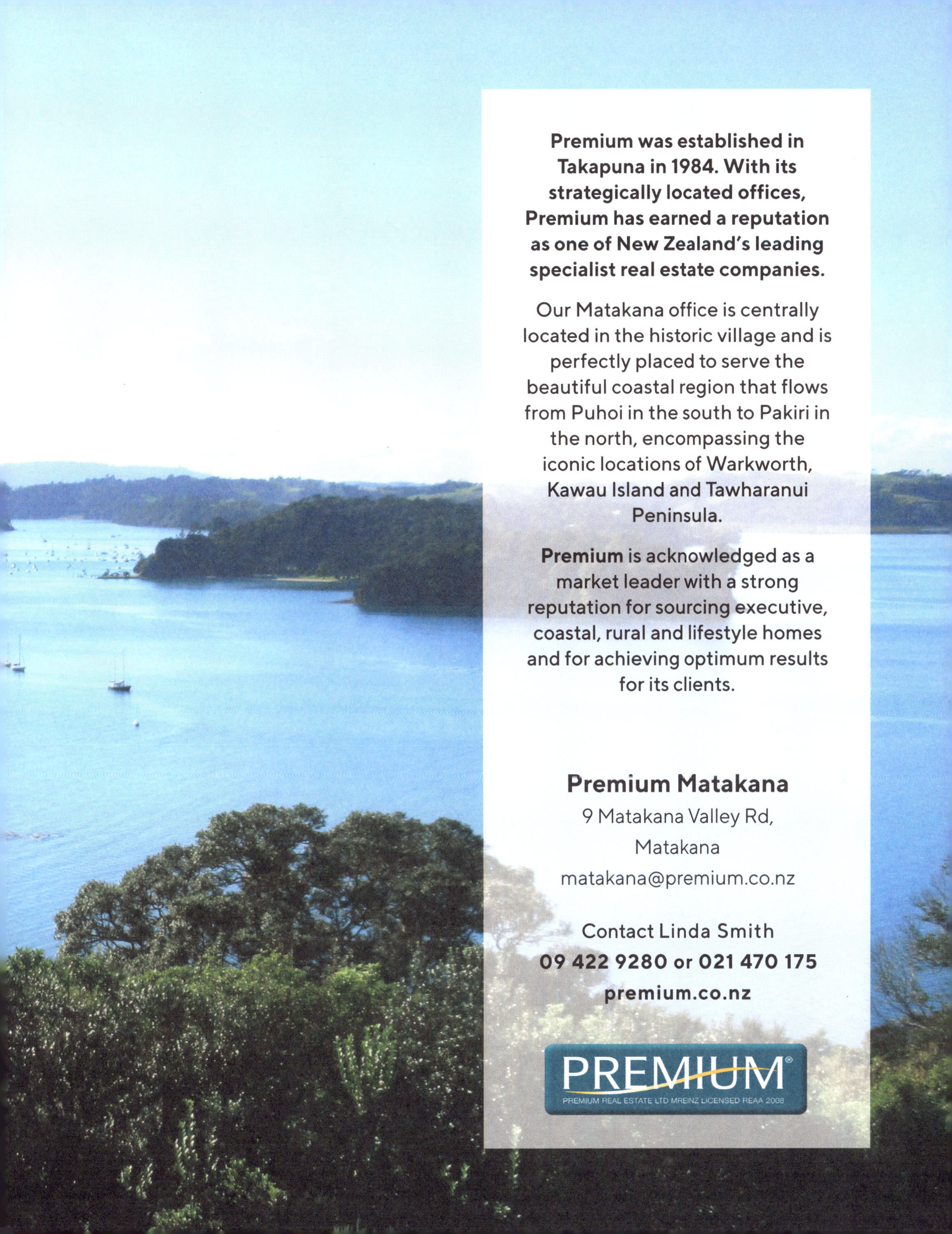
Premium was established in Takapuna in 1984. With its strategically located offices, Premium has earned a reputation as one of New Zealand's leading specialist real estate companies.
Our Matakana office is centrally located in the historic village and is perfectly placed to serve the beautiful coastal region that flows from Puhoi in the south to Pakiri in the north, encompassing the iconic locations of Warkworth, Kawau Island and Tawharanui Peninsula.
Premium is acknowledged as a market leader with a strong reputation for sourcing executive, coastal, rural and lifestyle homes and for achieving optimum results for its clients.
Premium Matakana
9 Matakana Valley Rd,
Matakana
matakana@premium.co.nz
Contact Linda Smith
09 422 9280 or 021 470 175
premium.co.nz
PREMIUM®
PREMIUM REAL ESTATE LTD MREINZ LICENSED REAA 2008

MATAVINO
HYPERION
MATAKANA
SCULPTUREUM
THE GABION
Countess
ROSÉ
RANSOM
ALBARIÑO
SALTINGS ESTATE
OBV
IMPOSTOR
2008
Coxhead Creek
rose
Gillman
NEW ZEALAND WINE
Brick Bay
MATAKANA
Pinot Gris
2016
HAWKS NEST
TAKATU
ROSE
MAHURANGI
Field Of Grace
CHARDONNAY
2014

MONARCH
ESTATE VINEYARD
Rosé
MATAKANA ESTATE
NEW ZEALAND

Board & Batten Interior Design
is your design destination. Providing a complete design service for new builds, refurbishments and renovations. Board & Batten encompasses all your interior and exterior design requirements.

Board and Batten Interior Design Ltd
897 Matakana Road
Matakana 0985
09 422 7891

deb@boardandbatten.co.nz
www.boardandbatten.co.nz

Board + Batten
Interior Design

Since 2014, the people of the Whangaripo Valley have come together at the end of summer to host their very own Wild Food Festival.

The popular event draws people from all over the Matakana region to the lush rural valley 'just over the hill'. It's an afternoon of old-fashioned family fun, with bell tents and bunting, hay bales and picnic blankets and the hard fought Valley Versus Village Tug-of-War.

Each dish must have an ingredient that is wild, caught, or foraged. Whether they're gathering cockles and cicada skins, harvesting watercress, catching eels or hunting pigs and peacock, Matakana's amateur chefs go all out in their quest to impress the judges.

In this chapter, we share ideas and recipes that we hope will inspire you to hunt, gather, forage and cook.

Hunt & Gather

Whangaripo Wild Food Festival

Wild duck Rillettes
Chickweed
Dandelion leaves
chestnuts
ginger
clover honey

Wild 'Valley'
Apple, peach & blackberry
Sangria

You're a winner!

ICE-CREAM
+ 'LOOS'

PAN SEARED VENISON STEAKS

WITH CAPSICUM SALSA & PARISIENNE POTATOES

The refreshing vibrant flavours of the salsa give the dish a sweet and sour element which balances out the slightly bitter aftertaste of the venison. The potatoes add a crunch to the dish.

Carmel Draper & Mark Griffiths

SERVES: 4 | PREP: 30 MINS + RESTING | COOK: 25 MINS | DIFFICULTY: MEDIUM

VENISON:

4 x 125g venison medallions

1 Tbsp Dijon mustard

Salt and pepper to taste

Olive oil

CAPSICUM SALSA:

1 red capsicum, chargrilled

1 yellow capsicum, chargrilled

2 tomatoes, blanched, quartered, seeds removed

1 red chilli

½ red onion

60ml red wine vinegar

60ml olive oil

50ml lime juice

5g coriander

Salt

PARISIENNE POTATOES:

500g potatoes, peeled

70g butter

70ml oil

Salt and Pepper to taste

For the venison, spread the medallions with the mustard, season with the salt and pepper then place on a suitably sized dish.

Pour a little olive oil over the steaks, cover with cling wrap and allow to rest for at least 30 minutes. Heat a pan over high heat, add a little oil to the pan followed by the steaks.

Cook the steaks to medium-rare, approximately 4-5 minutes either side depending on the thickness of the steak. Remove the pan from the heat, cover the steaks with foil and rest for 3 minutes.

For the salsa, chop the capsicums, tomatoes and onion into ½ cm cubes. Deseed the chilli and very finely chop.

Mix all the ingredients together in a bowl. Cover and leave at room temperature for at least 30 minutes. Taste and correct seasoning.

Preheat oven to 180°C.

Use a melon baller to make potato balls. Thoroughly dry with paper towels.

Heat a frying pan over medium heat, add the oil until it starts to shimmer.

Add the butter to the pan along with the potato balls, being careful not to splash the fat which is now hot.

Lightly season with salt and pepper. Gently toss the potatoes in the fat to give an even golden colour.

Place in the oven until cooked all the way through (8-10 minutes).

Serve the venison with the salsa on top and the potatoes on the side.

Notes: Leftover potatoes from making the potato balls can be cut and placed in a saucepan with salted boiling water and cooked for 10-12 minutes. Drain and add a small knob of butter, white pepper and then mash. That way nothing is wasted.

Annual olive pick

Deb Came

THE PEACOCK THAT WASN'T

Deb Came had helped organise the Whangaripo Wild Food Festival for three years before she decided to get serious about a dish of her own.

'I'd been so busy with the Festival that I had no time to cook,' says Deb. 'This time I wanted to concentrate on doing it properly.'

Deb had designs on a terrine, so husband Richard was dispatched across the road with instructions to rustle out one of the wild peacocks that dwell in the forest on his cousin's farm.

'The problem with peacocks is that they are fast and tricky'

The problem with peacocks, says Deb, is that they are 'fast and tricky'. After several fruitless hours traipsing through the undergrowth, Richard switched his sights to the wild turkeys that hang around at the back of their farm.

Happily for Deb, turkey is much easier to cook than peacock. 'Simply slice the turkey, lay it in the sausage meat, throw in some wild rosemary, garlic and a few free range eggs and wrap the whole thing up in bacon,' she says.

Add a balsamic blackberry glaze, and serve the terrine on fry bread with foraged watercress salsa, and you have an award-winning combination. Deb was rapt when her Wild Turkey Terrine took out both the People's Choice and the Overall Prize for 2017.

Deb, who grew up in Wellsford, is not a trained chef. 'I just love experimenting with food.'

With their three children almost grown, Deb's passion has led to an unexpected business venture, with the creation of Whangaripo Valley's first café, Whanga Eats, on a corner of the 300-acre dairy farm that has been in the Came family for over 100 years. 'Now it's my time.'

THE STABLES
RESTAURANT & BAR

WILD TURKEY TERRINE

This terrine can be made ahead, saving a lot of stress on a busy day. Before the Wild Food Festival I tested the recipe on my hungry teenage boys and they declared it a winner - what better recommendation could I have? Wild turkey adds a subtle gamey flavour, but you can substitute with store bought turkey or chicken.

Deb Came

SERVES: 6-8 | PREP: 12 HOURS | COOK: 3 HOURS | DIFFICULTY: MEDIUM

1kg turkey meat

500g sausage meat

Livers from the game meat, finely chopped (if you have any)

2 handfuls fresh breadcrumbs

1 egg

1 Tbsp thyme, finely chopped

2 Tbsp fresh rosemary, finely chopped

Rind of 1 lemon

2 garlic cloves, crushed

Splash of sherry or red wine

Salt and pepper

300g streaky bacon (to line the dish)

Cut turkey meat into small pieces or strips.

In a large mixing bowl, combine the sausage meat and the chopped livers from the turkey.

Next add breadcrumbs, egg, thyme, rosemary, lemon and garlic and then the wine or sherry. Season and mix everything together with your hands.

In a frying pan stir the turkey meat until nicely browned.

Line a loaf tin with the bacon strips.

Create layers using forcemeat (the sausage and liver mixture), then turkey, then forcemeat, then turkey and lastly a final layer of forcemeat.

Fold the bacon over the terrine and cover well with foil.

Preheat oven to 160°C.

Place terrine dish in a roasting pan half filled with hot water. Cook for 1½-3 hours.

Test with a skewer to see if it is cooked. If the skewer does not come out piping hot then it's not ready.

For the best possible texture and easy slicing, your terrine should be pressed. Use a brick wrapped in a plastic bag or similar to weight your terrine down.

Leave the terrine for several hours until completely cold, or overnight.

Notes: Serve in slices with green leaves, watercress salsa verde, blackberry balsamic glaze and fry bread (similar to pita).

RABBIT, LEEK & APPLE CIDER PIE

I grew up shooting wild rabbits on our farm in the Wairarapa. My mum would skin and joint them (she was tough) and put them in this delicious boozy pie. If you can't bring yourself to shoot a rabbit (or buy one from the butcher, already jointed) you can swap the rabbit out for chicken, goat or duck.

Katherine Norman

SERVES: 5 | PREP: 20-30 MINS + CHILLING | COOK: 1½ HOURS | DIFFICULTY: EASY

FILLING:

2 wild rabbits

225g plain flour

Salt and pepper to taste

1 large onion or two large leeks (or combo)

250g unsmoked streaky bacon

110g butter

Drizzle olive oil

1 apple (any size), peeled, sliced

2 garlic cloves, finely chopped

2½ tsp fresh thyme, chopped

400ml chicken stock

200ml apple cider

PASTRY:

225g plain flour

Pinch of salt

110g cold butter, cubed

5 Tbsp cold water

1 egg, lightly beaten

Firstly you'll need to joint the rabbits. Here's how it's done. Cut the hind quarters away from the body and separate the legs. Halve the leg joints. Cut the body horizontally through the backbone into two portions, stopping at the rib cage. Cut lengthways through the breastbone and divide the ribcage section in half. Flour and season the rabbit joints generously. If you are using chicken, just cut into 2.5cm cubes.

Add a little butter (25g) to a very large pot with a drizzle of olive oil to stop the butter from burning. Add the rabbit joints and fry for 5 minutes until browned and remove from the pot.

Finely slice the onion/leek and bacon and add to the pot and fry until browned.

Add the rabbit back to the pot along with the apple slices, finely chopped garlic and thyme and cook for a further 2 minutes. Then add the chicken stock and apple cider and simmer gently for 40 minutes. Turn off the heat and let the mixture cool down completely. Transfer to an ovenproof pie dish.

Preheat the oven to 180°C.

Whilst the mixture is cooling down you can make the pastry. I prefer shortcrust for this pie. You can use flaky or rough puff if you wish.

For 340g of shortcrust pastry (which will be more than enough to cover the pie dish), put the flour, salt and butter in a bowl and rub between your fingers to create a breadcrumb consistency. Then stir in a little water with a knife until the mixture becomes a dough. Wrap in cling wrap and chill for 20 minutes in the fridge.

Remove from the fridge and roll out over a floured work surface. Cover the pie filling with the pastry then press down the edges and trim away any excess. Brush pastry top with the beaten egg. Prick a few holes in the top with a fork to allow the steam to escape.

Bake for 25-30 minutes, or until the pastry is golden brown and the filling is piping hot.

Notes: I serve this with a big pile of steamed green beans. Happy eating!

SLOW BRAISED GOAT

WITH TURMERIC SPICED HUMMUS & CUMIN FLAT BREADS

This dish is perfect for whacking down in the middle of the table and getting stuck in. Goat adds a very special flavour to the dish. You could substitute the goat for lamb.

Will Michell

SERVES: 6 | PREP: 1 HOUR + SOAKING/MARINATING/PROVING | COOK: 4 HOURS | DIFFICULTY: HARD

HUMMUS:

500g dried chickpeas

2 garlic cloves

150ml extra virgin olive oil

150ml tahini paste

100ml lemon juice

2 garlic cloves, crushed

1 tsp ground cumin

1 tsp ground coriander

1½ tsp mild curry powder

1½ tsp ground turmeric

½ tsp chilli powder

½ tsp smoked paprika

GOAT:

2 Tbsp ground cumin

2 Tbsp ground ginger

2 Tbsp salt and black pepper

1 tsp ground cinnamon

1 tsp ground coriander

1 tsp ground allspice

½ tsp ground cloves

1 goat leg or 1kg of bone-in goat cuts

1 onion, roughly chopped

2 tomatoes, roughly chopped

1 litre chicken stock

FLATBREADS:

200g strong white flour

2 tsp ground cumin

1 tsp ground coriander

1 tsp fine salt

1½ tsp dried yeast

200ml warm water

To make the hummus, soak the chickpeas overnight in a large pot of cold water. Drain water off and cover with fresh cold water. Bring to the boil and cook until soft. Strain and keep half of the cooking water.

To confit the garlic, cover with some olive oil and slowly cook until cloves are soft, this will give a smoother and less harsh garlic taste.

Add all other ingredients and blend until smooth, adding some of the reserved cooking water as required to help make a smooth but firm hummus. Season with salt to taste. For a smoother hummus you can pass the hummus through a sieve, doing this whilst still hot will be easier and give a better result.

To prepare the meat, combine all spices and rub onto the goat and allow to marinate overnight.

Preheat oven to 150°C. Roughly chop onion and tomatoes and place in an oven tray. Place the goat on top of the vegetables and cover with stock. Wrap with foil and cook for around 3-4 hours until the meat is falling off the bone.

Remove from the oven and discard the onion. Pull meat off the bone and mix the shredded meat with the stock. Discard the bone.

For the flatbreads, sieve flour, cumin, coriander and salt into a large mixing bowl. In a separate jug, dissolve yeast in the water for 5 minutes.

Make a well in the flour mixture and pour water in, mixing with your hands. Turn dough out onto a floured bench and knead for around 7 minutes until a springy dough has formed. Place dough in a clean bowl and leave to rise for 1 hour.

Portion dough into 50g balls and roll to 5mm thickness and cook on a hot griddle pan or BBQ grill for 1 minute on each side, brushing with a little olive oil when you flip each one. The bread is ready when they start to puff up.

Notes: To serve, present the hummus in a large bowl with the hot shredded goat on top. Use a little of the stock to pour on top of the hummus for extra flavour and moisture. Serve flat breads on the side to dip into the hummus.

THE STABLES
RESTAURANT & BAR

Sweet mandarins from the Omaha Flats

Vicki Fanning

BEAUTY MEETS INDUSTRY

Frolic Headquarters is a curious blend of beauty and industry. At the heart of it all is Vicki Fanning – blow torch in hand, or arms covered in drying clay – long hair somehow miraculously clean.

Vicki grew up in the Mahurangi area, leaving at 19 to travel and study ceramics and later glass blowing and casting, supporting herself with gardening work and catering on film sets. 'You have to grow a lot of skills to fuel your art,' she says wryly.

'You have to grow a lot of skills to fuel your art'

Such practical skills are handy on the rural Matakana property she shares with partner and fellow artist, Mike Petre. Mike is renowned for his iconic black and white cattle paintings and as the designer behind local landmarks the Sawmill Brewery and The Vivian gallery, where both regularly exhibit.

Together, Mike and Vicki have renovated the original farmhouse and transformed bare paddocks into stunning gardens with groaning fruit trees and cheerful beds of brightly coloured dahlias.

Vicki launched Frolic Ceramics in 2013, when their son Sam started school. 'After years in catering, I inherently know what sizes and types of ceramics are needed,' she says. 'People always comment on how adaptable the pieces are.'

At Vicki's studio 'sale days', customers can purchase ceramic pieces paired with something special from the property – a jug of dahlias, or if you're lucky, some feijoa chutney.

Every autumn, Vicki, Mike and Sam invite a group of old friends to come and stay for the weekend, to help gather feijoas from the hedge, peel the fruit and roast the chutney. 'We play music and eat really well. It's a nice tradition.'

ROASTED FEIJOA & MANUKA CHUTNEY

On a busy day in the studio, cheese, chutney and crackers is my favourite lunch-on-the-run. Try this fragrant feijoa chutney with a mild goat's cheese (but even a slice of tasty cheese will do the trick!)

Vicki Fanning

SERVES: 10 JARS (APPROX) | PREP: 24 HOURS | COOK: 2-3 HOURS | DIFFICULTY: BASIC

3kg feijoas, peeled, roughly chopped

1kg red onions, finely chopped

8 green chillies, stems removed, julienned

2kg white sugar

2 tsp sea salt

300ml cider vinegar

5 large lemons, juiced, skins julienned

1 cinnamon quill

6 green cardamom pods, crushed (can add more if required)

2 tsp dried chilli flakes

1 small bunch manuka twigs with leaves

Mix all the ingredients together except for the manuka twigs, and leave in a covered bowl overnight.

The next day, add the manuka twigs and leaves, mix well and season if required.

Preheat oven to 180°C.

Place the ingredients in a non-corrosive roasting dish, put it in the oven and cook for 2-3 hours, stirring regularly.

The mixture is ready when the onions have caramelised and most of the liquid has evaporated.

Spoon into very hot sterilised jars and seal.

Notes: The chutney is great with roast lamb or cold meat cuts and also works well with cheese and crackers.

Make sure you also sterilise your lids.

CRAZY COCKLES

WITH WILD PESTO & AMARANTH SEED FLOWER

This recipe was the winner of the People's Choice Kids category at the 2017 Whangaripo Wild Food Festival.

Flynn & Samara Powell

SERVES: 6 | PREP: 5-10 MINS + FORAGING | COOK: 10-15 MINS | DIFFICULTY: BASIC

Cockles (as many as you can find)

¼ cup white wine

2 cups spinach

2 cups nasturtium leaves

3 garlic cloves, chopped

½ cup cashews

½ tsp salt

¼ tsp black pepper

½ cup olive oil

¼ cup parmesan

Amaranth seed flower (optional but has a wonderful parsley-like flavour)

Steam open cockles in white wine, remove from their shells and put aside.

To make the pesto, add spinach, nasturtium leaves, garlic and cashews into a food processor and blend for 5-10 seconds.

Add salt, pepper and olive oil, blend until all ingredients have been incorporated.

Add the parmesan and pulse for 5-10 seconds to combine.

Serve in small dishes or shells with a dollop of pesto and a couple of cockles on top.

Garnish with amaranth seed flower.

BLACK OLIVE TAPENADE

This is a very easy last minute recipe to put together that will always impress your guests.

Robin & Simon Barclay

SERVES: 1½ CUPS | PREP: 40 MINS | NO COOK

1½ cups Kalamata olives

3 Tbsp capers, drained

3 garlic cloves, coarsely chopped

¼ cup fresh herbs, e.g. parsley, rosemary and thyme, chopped

8 anchovy fillets, coarsely chopped

Juice of 1 lemon

⅓ cup extra virgin olive oil

Remove olive stones using an olive stoner or by squashing the olives with the flat side of a knife.

Place the olives, capers, garlic, herbs, anchovies and lemon juice in a food processor and mix until just combined. While still mixing, gradually add the olive oil in a thin, steady stream.

Mix until well combined but be careful not to over-process as the tapenade should retain some texture.

Adjust the flavour if necessary by adding a little salt or additional lemon juice.

Place the tapenade in a serving bowl and leave to stand for at least 1 hour to allow flavours to infuse.

Serve at room temperature.

BEETROOT & BALSAMIC RELISH

This is a wonderful relish which I use on salads and cold meats. It's also fantastic on homemade burgers.

Josie Hyslop

SERVES: 4 X 450G JARS | PREP: 30 MINS | COOK: 40 MINS | DIFFICULTY: BASIC

750g beetroot, peeled, grated

1 onion, chopped

2 cups balsamic vinegar

1 cup water

2½ cups sugar

3 tsp yellow mustard seeds

2 whole cloves

5cm piece orange rind (peel with a potato peeler)

Salt and black pepper

Place all ingredients into a large pot, cover and bring to the boil.

Cook for 30 minutes or until beetroot is soft and the liquid has reduced and thickened slightly.

Spoon into hot sterilised jars and seal.

Amber Rose

FORAGING FOR BEGINNERS

It's a long way from Kaiwaka to the celebrity kitchens of London, but for chef Amber Rose, the connection is clear. 'My childhood has inspired everything I do.'

Amber's mother Kay Baxter was a pioneer of organic farming in New Zealand and co-founded the Koanga Institute, a not-for-profit organisation dedicated to the preservation of heritage fruit trees and vegetable plants.

'Food was something we grew, farmed and foraged,' says Amber. 'We caught fish in the Kaipara, gathered mushrooms, and picked berries off the totara tree. Mum preserved, dried, salted, smoked, cured, baked bread, harvested honey from her own hives and even made candles from the beeswax. She has the Kiwi can-do attitude to the extreme!'

Amber absorbed everything. 'I'm not officially trained as a chef, but I had a training people would only dream of.'

'Food was something we grew, farmed and foraged'

In her 20s, Amber went travelling, eventually landing in London, where she served up wholefood meals and sweet treats for health conscious celebrities like Kate Moss and Gwyneth Paltrow. She developed an interest in food styling, and created her first books, the international bestseller *Love Bake Nourish*, followed by *The Wholefood Pantry*.

In 2016, Amber suddenly felt the need to bring son Ollie home. That journey inspired a new book, *Wild Delicious*. 'It's about how I grew up eating from the wild, and coming home.'

One Saturday in Matakana, she got chatting to local food stylist Kate Arbuthnot and a new professional collaboration was born. As well as preparing and styling food for magazine shoots, the pair now host bespoke seasonal foraging workshops at Totem Retreat in the Whangaripo Valley.

Amber's

FOUR RULES OF FORAGING

1. Pick where there is an abundance , and leave more than you take.
2. Know where you are foraging and always seek permission first.
3. Choose a clean spot – don't forage from a filthy roadside or polluted river.
4. Know what you're picking – if you're not 100 per cent sure, don't eat it.

THE STABLES
RESTAURANT & BAR

PRESERVED FIGS

Figs have a unique, sweet taste, soft and chewy texture and are littered with slightly crunchy, edible seeds. Fresh figs are delicate and perishable, and this recipe provides a way to preserve and enjoy them year round without having to dry them.

Lauraine Jacobs

SERVES: 3-6 JARS (DEPENDING ON SIZE) | PREP: 2 DAYS + 7 DAYS TO MATURE | COOK: 1 HOUR | DIFFICULTY: EASY

3kg fresh figs (about 30-40)

1 litre water

1 cup salt

Cloves

1 litre white wine vinegar

1½ kg sugar

1 cinnamon stick

3 pieces of root ginger, each 2cm, thinly sliced

1 Tbsp allspice

Soak the figs overnight in the water and salt.

Drain the figs and place a clove in each fig.

Combine vinegar and sugar in a pot with spices and bring to the boil.

Add figs and simmer gently for one hour.

Turn off heat, cover the pot and leave overnight.

Place the figs in sterilised jars and boil the remaining liquid until syrupy.

Pour the liquid over the figs in the jars and leave to stand for an hour or so to allow the figs to absorb the liquid, then top up the jars with the remaining liquid.

Cover tightly with screw top lids and allow the flavour to mature for at least one week before serving.

Notes: The preserved figs are particularly delicious when paired with meat (especially duck) or on a cheeseboard with a nice soft goat cheese and oat crackers.

Charlies' luscious strawberries and gelato are summertime favourites

BERRY & GIN JAM

This recipe comes from Ripe Recipes, a cookbook published by the Ripe Deli in Grey Lynn. No one at the Deli can remember quite how the gin came to be in the jam, but everyone agrees the result is divine.

Cate Ashwell

SERVES: 1½ LITRES | PREP: 20 MINS + SOAK OVERNIGHT | COOK: 40 MINS | DIFFICULTY: EASY

1kg berries, fresh or frozen

Juice of 2-3 lemons (optional)

¼ cup gin

1kg white sugar

Remove any stalks from the berries and soak overnight in lemon juice and gin.

In a large heavy based pot, combine the berries and sugar.

On a low to medium heat, slowly bring to a boil and continue boiling for about 20 minutes. Stir occasionally to avoid sticking.

The jam is ready when the mixture has thickened a little.

Drop spoonfuls onto a saucer to check the setting point – push it with your finger and if it wrinkles it is set. If you own a sugar thermometer, the setting temperature for jams and jellies is 105°C.

Pour hot jam into sterilised jars and seal.

LIMONCELLO

One for the grownups, Limoncello is easy to make and can also be a great gift. Keep a bottle in the freezer and serve it chilled in shot glasses as an after dinner digestif, or in tall glasses topped with soda or Prosecco for a refreshing aperitif.

From the Kitchen of Carlton Party Hire

SERVES: 2 LITRES | PREP: 10 MINS + 4 DAYS STEEPING | COOK: 10 MINS | DIFFICULTY: BASIC

10 lemons, unwaxed, organic, with a nice thick skin

1 litre vodka

800g caster sugar

1 litre water

Peel the zest from the lemons with a vegetable peeler, taking care not to include any white pith.

Put the zest in a large clean jar and pour over the vodka.

Cover with a tightly fitting lid and leave for 4 days in a cool, dark place, giving the jar a shake each day.

Dissolve the sugar and water in a pot, bring to the boil and boil for a few minutes until syrupy.

Strain the lemony vodka from the zest and mix with the sugar syrup.

Bottle and store in the freezer.

Trish Allen

PERMACULTURE PARADISE

When asked, 'Why sauerkraut?' Trish Allen says simply, 'I married an Austrian!'

In the 1970s, Trish was living in Vienna and working for the United Nations, when she briefly met Joe Polaischer.

Seven years later Joe was hitchhiking around New Zealand and on the last day of that trip, decided to give Trish a call. 'I invited him for dinner – and he stayed six weeks! We got married two years later.'

The pair shared a passion for growing food without chemicals, and together, discovered permaculture. 'Permaculture is about holistic living, working with nature not against. Care for the earth, care for people, share resources and limit consumption,' says Trish. 'It covers everything – energy efficient housing, minimising waste. All of the good things that look after our planet.'

'Permaculture is about holistic living, working with nature not against'

In 1988 the couple found 50 acres of pest-ridden, rundown land in Matakana Valley and transformed it into Rainbow Valley Farm, a world-famous permaculture hive of green-fingered industry and education.

The pair were instrumental in helping found the Matakana Village Farmers' Market, and had a produce stall for several years. When Joe died suddenly in 2008 Trish reluctantly accepted the farm was too much, but only after breaking her ankle and spending three months in a wheelchair. 'Finally I understood, it was time to let it go.'

Now settled on 'a quarter acre of permaculture paradise' in the village, Trish continues to pioneer eco projects, like co-founding the Matakana Community Garden, which transformed a waste area beside the Village Hall into a space where locals come together to weed, plant, compost and share in the harvest.

SAUERKRAUT

I grew to love sauerkraut while living in Vienna and only learned about the health benefits later. Sauerkraut is full of vitamin C and as it's probiotic, promotes healthy gut flora which is vital for a good immune system. Eat a little every day with a meal.

Trish Allen

SERVES: 40 | PREP: 30 MINS | NO COOKING | DIFFICULTY: BASIC

1 medium cabbage, cored and shredded

1 Tbsp sea salt

1 Tbsp caraway seeds (optional)

In a bowl, mix cabbage with sea salt and pound with a wooden pounder to release juices. Add caraway seeds and mix through. Pack into a large clean glass jar and press down firmly to remove air. Place a large outer cabbage leaf on top and continue pressing down until juices come up and cover the cabbage. Put a weight on top to keep the cabbage submerged – a small jar of water or stones works well.

Cover and leave at room temperature for about 2-3 weeks before putting it in the fridge.

Notes: This is an anaerobic process, keep your vegetables covered with liquid, ensuring they have no contact with air.

Keep your sauerkraut where you can see it, taste regularly and refrigerate when it is at its optimum.

Remove any scum/mould or debris from the top as soon as you see it. If there is red mould, throw it out and start again.

Warmer temperatures make fermentation happen faster. More salt makes the process slower, less salt makes the process faster, but if using less than recommended, there is the risk of spoilage.

SOUS VIDE DUCK BREAST

& WILD MUSHROOMS

Sous Vide cooking is science, this is the perfect duck breast.

From the Kitchen of the Stables

SERVES: 1 | PREP: 30 MINS | COOK: 2 HOURS | DIFFICULTY: HARD

200g duck breast

RISOTTO:

Butter or oil

150g onions, finely chopped

15g garlic

50g Arborio rice

200ml chicken stock

100ml Rocland – Chocolate Box Shiraz

60g wild mushrooms

50g butter

25g Parmigiano Reggiano, grated

DUCK CRUMB:

Trimming from duck breast

15g crispy dried shallots

ORANGE GEL:

2 oranges

Agar – 3% of total yield

Valrhona chocolate

To prepare and cook the duck breast, trim the fat, score the skin, season and cook at 57°C for 2 hours in a Sous Vide.

To finish, place the duck skin down in a hot pan and render the fat until the duck is crispy. Slice the duck breast.

For the risotto, heat some butter or oil in a pan, add the onions and garlic and cook until soft.

Add the rice and stir until coated with the butter/oil.

Deglaze the pan with red wine and slowly add stock one ladle at a time. Once the stock has been absorbed, add more. Continue adding stock until the rice is al dente. Add the mushrooms, butter and Parmigiano Reggiano and stir.

To make the duck crumb, fry the duck fat trimmings to render the fat from them, strain and blend with crispy shallots.

For the orange gel, boil the oranges three times for 20 minutes each time, using fresh water for each boil.

Drain, blend and pass through a sieve. Add the agar and set in the fridge for 20 minutes. Once it has set, blend and pass through the sieve once again.

To serve, place the risotto off centre on the plate. Place sliced duck breast on top. Garnish with orange gel, duck crumb and grated Valrhona chocolate.

Notes: You can find agar and Valrhona chocolate at specialty grocery stores.

When using agar, you need to weigh what you are going to thicken (the yield) and then calculate 3% for the amount of agar to add. In this case, you need to weigh the orange mix for the gel recipe.

The Stables Restaurant & Bar
Located at the Matakana Country Park on the main road to Leigh, just minutes from the Matakana Village. Enjoy outdoor dining with stylish and panoramic views of the stunning landscape and equestrian arena, or dine indoors in the spacious dining room with large glass doors and fireplaces at each end.

The Stables Restaurant is great for a casual lunch or dinner. It is also a perfect venue for large parties, functions, corporate events and weddings. With ample parking, a playground and activities for children, an art gallery, gym and craft shop on-site, there is something for everyone to enjoy. The Stables is the destination for a great dining experience.

The Stables
09 422 7360
FB stablesmatakana
IG @stablesmatakana
enquiries@stablesmatakana.co.nz
www.stablesmatakana.co.nz

THE STABLES
RESTAURANT & BAR

Desserts

Whangateau Folk Club

On the last Monday of every month, the timber floorboards of the 120-year-old Whangateau Hall thump to the soulful, heart-stirring tunes of the local folk club. It's a place where everyone is welcome and anyone can step up to the mic.

Established in 2014 by a group of passionate music lovers, the club is led by Ti Point dynamo Jenine Abarbanel, lead singer and double bass player for 'The Pipi Pickers'. 'I'm a huge fan of folk music, I'm also big on anything that gets people away from their TVs and out mingling with their neighbours.'

The Folk Club regularly hosts world-class independent folk acts attracted to Whangateau by the warmth of the audience and the wonderful acoustics of the hall. We think the traditional half-time cuppa has something to do with it as well.

In this chapter you'll find sweet treats and sumptuous desserts fit for every joyful occasion.

WHANGATEAU
Ascension
WINE ESTATE

SOUTHERN PECAN PIE

This is a traditional Thanksgiving dessert recipe passed down from our American grandparents. It is an autumnal crowd pleaser for those who don't like pumpkin pie, and the maple syrup gives it extra flavour.

The Satterthwaite Family

SERVES: 12 | PREP: 1 HOUR | COOK: 50-70 MINS | DIFFICULTY: EASY

PIE CRUST:

3 cups plain flour

1 tsp salt

¾ cup vegetable shortening

¾ cup salted butter, cut into pieces, very chilled

4 Tbsp chilled water

1 Tbsp vodka or gin, chilled

1 egg, lightly beaten

FILLING:

1 cup granulated sugar

3 Tbsp brown sugar

½ tsp salt

1 cup maple syrup (or corn syrup but grade A maple has better flavour)

⅓ cup melted salted butter

2 tsp vanilla extract

3 whole eggs, beaten

2 heaped cups pecans, chopped

First cut and measure the butter and water/alcohol and put it in the freezer while you gather all the ingredients.

To make the pie crust, mix the flour and salt in a bowl. Add the vegetable shortening and chilled salted butter. Work the butter and shortening into the flour using a dough cutter or clean hands until the mixture resembles tiny pebbles. The colder the butter the better, you want solid pieces of butter to get a flaky crust.

Drop in 2 tablespoons of cold water with one tablespoon of the alcohol. Stir until just combined, add the rest of the water, then use your hands to form the dough. Divide the dough in half and chill in the fridge until needed. (You will only need one half for this recipe, reserve the other half for another time or use to decorate with a lattice design or autumn leaf shapes on top).

Preheat oven to 180°C.

To make the filling, mix the granulated sugar, brown sugar, salt, maple syrup, butter, vanilla and eggs together in a bowl.

Roll out one dough half on a lightly floured surface to fit your pie pan. Pour half of the pecans in the bottom of the unbaked pie shell. Pour the filling mixture over the top. Place the remaining pecans on top of the pie for decoration or skip if covering with pastry. Cover the top and crust lightly with foil.

Bake the pie for 30 minutes. Remove the foil, and then continue baking for 20 minutes, being careful not to burn the crust or pecans. The pie should not be overly jiggly when you remove it from the oven. If it shakes a lot, cover with foil and bake for an additional 20 minutes or until set. Actual baking time will vary depending on whether you use fan bake or your oven type.

Allow to cool for several hours or overnight (which is even better for taste and ease of serving). Serve in thin slivers with freshly whipped cream.

Notes: If you don't have shortening, substitute with butter.

APPLE SNOW PIE

This is a favourite dessert recipe that I modified so that I could still enjoy it after becoming gluten free. It isn't overly sweet so the tartness of the Granny Smiths is a great combination with the sweet meringue.

The Macfarlane Family

SERVES: 6-8 | PREP: 20-25 MINS | COOK: 40 MINS | DIFFICULTY: MEDIUM

PASTRY CRUST:

1 cup ground almonds

1 cup buckwheat flour

1-2 tsp ground cinnamon

Zest of 1 lemon

2 Tbsp honey

100g unsalted butter, softened

1-2 Tbsp water

PIE FILLING:

6-8 Granny Smith apples, peeled, sliced

50g butter

Grated zest and juice of 1 lemon

2 Tbsp brown sugar

1 tsp vanilla bean paste

MERINGUE TOPPING:

4 egg whites, at room temperature

¾ cup caster sugar

Preheat oven to 180°C.

Grease pie flan dish (detachable base is preferable).

To make the pastry, pulse all pastry ingredients except water in a food processor until mixture resembles fine breadcrumbs.

Add water 1 tablespoon at a time until the dough starts to come together in a ball.

Press mixture into flan dish. Prick pastry with a fork.

Bake for 8-10 minutes or until slightly crispy and leave to cool completely.

To make the apple filling, put all ingredients into a fry pan and simmer on low to medium heat to soften the apples. Stir occasionally. Set aside to cool.

To make the meringue, beat the egg whites until they hold firm peaks, then add the sugar gradually and continue to beat until glossy.

Put apple filling on top of pie crust. Pile meringue mixture on top of apples, covering the apples, taking the meringue to the pastry rim.

Bake for 15 minutes or until the meringue is browned.

Serve with cream or vanilla bean custard.

'"CHEESE" CAKE

We love food and are passionate about healthy eating but it has to be simple to make. This one is loved by our kids (not always easy with four of them as it has to be gluten and dairy free) and it looks stunning with the red topping of raspberries or bright yellow if you decide to use mango instead.

The Fox Family

SERVES: 6-8 | PREP: 30 MINS + CHILLING | NO COOK | DIFFICULTY: EASY

BASE:

150g almonds (or pecans or walnuts)

50g pumpkin seeds

12 pitted dates

8 Tbsp desiccated coconut

2 tsp ground cinnamon

3 Tbsp coconut oil, melted

'CREAM CHEESE' FILLING:

100g cashew nuts

100g sunflower seeds

3 pitted dates

Juice of 1 lemon

3 Tbsp coconut oil, melted

1 tsp vanilla essence

Pinch of salt

TOPPING (COULIS):

200g frozen mixed berries

Juice and rind of 1 lime or lemon

Grease a 20cm springform tin with coconut oil and line with baking paper.

To make the base, mix the nuts, seeds, dates, coconut and cinnamon in a food processor until it forms a dough. Add the coconut oil and mix again.

Press the dough into the tin with a fork or spoon.

Let it rest in the fridge while you make the filling.

Soak the cashews, sunflower seeds and dates in warm water for 5 minutes to make them soft. Drain.

Mix cashew nuts, sunflower seeds, dates, lemon juice, melted coconut oil, vanilla essence and salt in the food processor until you get a smooth consistency. If it's too thick, add some water.

Pour the filling over the base and put it in the fridge for a few hours to set.

For the topping, mix the berries with lemon juice and rind in the food processor then pour it over the "cheese" cake just before serving.

Notes: You can add melted dark chocolate over the top, or serve with fresh mint leaves.

You can use pureed mango for the topping instead of berries.

CHOCOLATE ESPRESSO TART

We love this tart because it's decadent and delicious at the same time as being healthy. It's perfect if you have anyone with dairy or wheat allergies.

Rachel O'Malley

SERVES: 8-14 | PREP: 30 MINS + SOAKING + FREEZING | COOK: 13 MINS | DIFFICULTY: MEDIUM

CRUST:

1½ cups rolled oats, divided

¾ cup hazelnuts

¼ cup coconut oil

3 Tbsp maple syrup

¼ tsp fine-grain sea salt

FILLING:

1½ cups cashews, soaked for at least 4 hours

¾ cup pure maple syrup

½ cup coconut oil

⅓ cup cocoa powder (or raw cacao powder)

⅓ cup dark chocolate chips, melted

2 tsp pure vanilla extract (or seeds of ½ vanilla bean)

½ tsp fine-grain sea salt

½ tsp espresso powder (optional)

Shaved dark chocolate (optional)

Coconut flakes (optional)

CASHEW CREAM:

½ cup cashews, soaked for at least 4 hours

3 Tbsp maple syrup

4 Tbsp water

Couple pinches of sea salt

Preheat oven to 180°C. Lightly grease a 23cm pie dish with coconut oil. Blend ½ cup of the rolled oats on high until you have a rough flour and set aside. Process the hazelnuts until they have the texture of sand. Add coconut oil, maple syrup, salt and oat flour. Process again until the mixture sticks together. Add the remaining cup of oats and pulse until the oats are roughly chopped.

If the dough does not stick together, add more maple syrup or process a bit longer. Crumble the dough over the base of the pie dish and firmly press into the bottom and sides. Pierce base with a fork. Bake the crust, uncovered, for 10-13 minutes, until lightly golden. Remove from the oven and set aside to cool.

For the filling, drain and rinse the cashews. In a blender, combine the cashews, maple syrup, oil, cocoa powder, melted chocolate, vanilla, salt and espresso powder (if using). Blend on high until completely smooth, adding a tablespoon of almond milk if necessary. Pour the filling into the prepared crust, smoothing evenly. Garnish with shaved chocolate and/or coconut flakes, if desired. Freeze uncovered for a couple of hours, then cover with foil and freeze overnight, or a minimum of 4-6 hours, until the pie sets.

To make the cashew cream, drain and rinse cashews. Blend all ingredients on high until completely smooth. Store in the fridge. Remove the pie from the freezer and let it sit for 10 minutes before slicing. This tart is meant to be served frozen.

Serve the tart with the cashew cream and finely chopped chocolate, if desired, but it's also fantastic on its own.

Gay Smith

A COMMUNITY SERVICE STATION

After a busy day at Gull Matakana, Gay Smith picks up a box of donated fresh produce ready for her next shift: sorting food for Warkworth Food Rescue.

A longstanding member of the Kowhai Coast Lions Club and Matakana Community Group, Gay helped establish the scheme that collects excess perishable food from retailers, commercial food producers and backyard gardeners, for distribution to those in need.

'In the first 20 months, we sorted over 30 tonnes of food that would have gone to waste and delivered it to organisations like Homebuilders, Women's Refuge and the Women's Centre,' Gay says proudly.

'It feels good to give back '

'We always need fresh produce, so anyone can drop fruit and veggies to the garage and I'll take it to Food Rescue,' she continues. 'In our business, people are always giving us their money, so it feels good to give back. I just want to help people as much as I can.'

Food Rescue is the latest project in a long history of community service that began when Gay and her husband Mike came north in 1983 and purchased the little garage in the village, converting the old tyre bay (now the Rusty Tui) into the family home.

Gay found herself at the centre of village life. 'I knew all my customers by name and would lend things from my pantry - or even my wardrobe - if they got caught short,' says Gay. 'People would tell me all about their grandchildren and then bring them in to meet me. The place is a lot busier now, but I enjoy being part of a vibrant village.' This bread and butter pudding is Gay's go-to dish for community pot-luck dinners.

APRICOT JAM BREAD & BUTTER PUDDING

My generation was brought up on bread and butter pudding. I always make this for committee events as for some reason, the men just love it. The apricot jam adds a yummy sweetness, or try marmalade for a lemony twist.

Gay Smith

SERVES: 6 | PREP: 30 MINS | COOK: 40 MINS | DIFFICULTY: BASIC

- **8 slices white bread**
- **Apricot jam**
- **300ml cream**
- **300ml milk**
- **6 eggs, beaten**
- **½ cup caster sugar**
- **1 tsp vanilla essence**
- **Cinnamon (optional)**

Preheat oven to 160°C.

Butter 8 slices of bread and spread with apricot jam.

Roll the bread up with the jam on the inside, cut each roll in half and stand cut side up (with the crust on the bottom of the dish) in a 16cm x 24cm ovenproof dish. Repeat with each slice.

Combine the cream, milk, eggs, sugar and vanilla in a large jug or bowl and very slowly pour the mixture over the bread.

Stand for 20 minutes before baking to allow the custard to be soaked into the bread. Sprinkle with cinnamon if you wish.

Bake the pudding for approximately 40 minutes or until a thin bladed knife inserted into the centre comes out clean.

Notes: I use ½ cup of sugar but you can use slightly more (¾ cup).

I add as many slices of bread as I need to fill the dish I am using and adjust the quantities of the custard ingredients accordingly.

I have also sprinkled through dark chocolate chips and this is rather yummy. Serve with ice cream, yoghurt, cream and/or fresh fruit salad.

LEMON HEAVEN

This was my 'Fairy Godmother's' go-to dessert. When I was living in London, I would escape to her cottage in Surrey for the weekend when I needed a break and some TLC. She used to cook me delicious home cooked dinners and we'd often finish with Lemon Heaven and whatever fruit was in season. It was heaven!

Hannah Anderson

SERVES: 4-6 | PREP: 2 HOURS | NO COOKING | DIFFICULTY: BASIC

395g can condensed milk

3 large lemons

300ml whipping cream

Fresh raspberries or strawberries to serve

Lemon curd to serve (optional)

Mix the can of condensed milk with the rind and juice of 3 lemons.

Whip 300ml of cream and fold into the lemon mixture.

Place in the fridge to set for at least two hours.

Notes: Lemon Heaven can be made as one large serving or it can be divided into individual serves.

It is particularly delicious served with fresh raspberries or strawberries.

COOKIES 'N' CREAM AFFOGATO

This affogato looks lovely in a glass, feels like a special treat and is easy to throw together at the last minute. Everyone loves pouring hot coffee over ice cream and watching it melt, and the espresso can be swapped for hot chocolate to make it suitable for kids.

Madison Clifton

SERVES: 4 | PREP: 15 MINS | NO COOKING | DIFFICULTY: EASY

200ml or 4 double shots espresso

2 chocolate brownies of choice

1 litre tub Cookies n Cream Ice Cream

3-4 Tbsp maple syrup

Nutmeg, grated

Set 4 glasses or jars on a serving tray ready to be filled.

Prepare your espresso and put aside to cool. Roughly chop brownies and place a tablespoon into the bottom of each glass.

Place 2 scoops of ice cream into each of the glasses.

Pour 50ml of espresso into each glass, then spoon maple syrup over the ice cream.

Garnish with grated nutmeg and brownie crumbs.

Finding solace on the Whangateau sandbars

INDIVIDUAL SUMMER PUDDINGS

Summer pudding is a quintessentially English dish that went out of fashion but has come back with a vengeance. It can be found in trendy London restaurants. Don't be put off by the bread, give it a go!

The Taylor Family

SERVES: 8 | PREP: 20 MINS + CHILL OVERNIGHT | COOK: 5 MINS | DIFFICULTY: MEDIUM

1kg mixed berries - raspberries, blueberries, redcurrants, blackberries and strawberries, plus extra to serve

50g caster sugar

4 Tbsp Crème de Cassis (or water)

Large loaf white bread (approx 800g), sliced

Strip stalks from the berries and hull strawberries. Place berries in a non-stick pot with sugar and cassis or water. Heat pan until it starts to sizzle. Cook over a medium heat for 2-3 minutes or until the fruits start to soften.

Stir gently, then cool to room temperature. Strain fruit through a sieve into a bowl for about 10 minutes or until the juices stop dripping.

Have 8 small cups (about 200ml capacity) ready.

Using 2 cutters (approximately 10cm and 6cm, but check against the tops and bottoms of your cups), cut out 8 bread rounds of each size. Cut the crusts off 8 more slices and slice in half. The strips should be the same depth as the cups.

Dip the small rounds of bread into the juices you set aside and press into the cups.

Dip the straight slices in the juice and press around the sides.

Spoon in the fruits, pressing down with the back of a spoon.

Dip the last bread rounds into the juice; press down on top. Chill overnight.

When ready to serve, loosen bread tops with the tip of a knife. Hold a small plate over the pudding, then turn upside down and shake well. The puddings should slip out, if not loosen the sides gently with a knife.

Pour remaining juice over the tops of the puddings and decorate with the remaining fruit.

Notes: Serve with cream, ice cream or clotted cream.

Ascension
WINE ESTATE

MERINGUE STACK WITH RASPBERRY COULIS

This dessert is a fancy twist on traditional pavlova and perfect for a special celebration, or a long lunch in the orchard. It doesn't really matter if your pavlova layers turn out less than perfect - simply pile on the cream, berries and coulis for a show stopping dessert.

Christine Sheehy

SERVES: 8-10 | PREP: 1 HOUR + COOLING | COOK: 1 HOUR | DIFFICULTY: HARD

MERINGUE:

6 egg whites

1¾ cups caster sugar

1½ tsp vinegar

3 tsp cornflour

1½ tsp vanilla extract or essence

RASPBERRY COULIS:

2 cups raspberries (fresh or frozen)

¼ cup caster sugar

Juice of ½ lemon

RICH CREAM:

300ml cream

½ cup crème fraîche (or more to taste)

1½ tsp vanilla extract or essence

GARNISH:

Fresh berries

Mint

Rose petals

Preheat oven to 140°C.

Line two baking trays with foil or baking paper and draw three circles with diameters of 20cm, 15cm and 10cm.

Beat egg whites on medium speed, until soft peaks form. Continue beating, while you slowly add the sugar 1 tablespoon at a time. This should take around 8-10 minutes.

Add vinegar, cornflour and vanilla extract. Beat on high until meringue is glossy and stiff peaks form (3 to 5 minutes).

Spread onto the circles using the back of a spoon.

Place meringue in the oven, reduce heat to 100°C and bake until crisp and dry to the touch, approximately 1 hour (depending on your oven).

Turn off the oven and leave meringues in the oven to cool for at least one hour.

Place raspberries, sugar and lemon juice in a saucepan. Simmer, crushing berries with a fork occasionally, until the liquid is reduced by half (about 15 minutes). Press through a sieve to remove seeds. If it's too thick to pour easily, add a little water. Set aside to cool.

Whip cream until soft peaks form. Fold in crème fraîche with a spoon.

Add vanilla and whip gently to firm peaks, ready to spread on the meringue.

To assemble (just before serving), dollop 1 tablespoon of rich cream on the serving plate to hold the meringue in place. Place the largest meringue on the plate. Spread with cream, a drizzle of coulis and a scattering of berries.

Repeat for the second and third layer.

Drizzle coulis over the top and scatter with berries, mint and petals.

Notes: Coulis keeps in the fridge for up to a week. Raspberries give a gorgeous bright red colour, but you can also use mixed berries, or strawberries.

Rural hinterland in the Whangaripo Valley

Kate Arbuthnot

ON THE WILD SIDE

Food stylist Kate Arbuthnot and her husband Dave Hassan knew little of the Whangaripo Valley when they came north in search of a rural property. 'We found this homestead made from rough-sawn kauri grown on the land, and fell in love,' says Kate.

No matter that the rambling house was home to farm animals - Kate says simply, 'We did all that up.'

Once settled, Kate was delighted to discover a valley rich in resourceful and quirky characters, with a strong love of hunting and fishing. 'The community is so vibrant, that's what I love about this area.'

When Auckland Council threatened to close the Whangaripo Hall for lack of use, it was time to act. 'I knew instantly that we had to do a wild food festival,' says Kate. 'The area just lends itself to an event like that.'

So the talented foodies and creatives of the Whangaripo Hall Committee got to work and launched the festival in 2014. 'It really took off because it appealed to everybody: farmers, Matakana foodies, hunters and gatherers. People were cooking up big paellas outside the hall and making creations from whatever they'd been diving for that day.'

'I knew instantly that we had to do a wild food festival'

As for the most memorable dishes? 'Nasturtium ice cream, chocolate-dipped cicadas, kawakawa shortbread, snail paella and deep-fried crickets in a tempura batter' says Kate. 'It took me weeks to forage enough of those crickets mind you!'

Luckily all that foraging paid off. Now that Kate and Dave have relocated to Snells Beach, the villa provides the perfect setting for foraging workshops hosted by Kate and chef Amber Rose.

Ascension
WINE ESTATE

ROSE PANNA COTTA

WITH POACHED TAMARILLOS & CARAMELISED WHITE CHOCOLATE

This recipe comes from my colleague, food writer Delaney Mes. The rosewater gives the panna cotta a subtle flavour, and the tartness of the tamarillo cuts through the sweetness of the white chocolate.

Kate Arbuthnot

SERVES: 6 | PREP: 20 MINS + CHILL OVERNIGHT | COOK: 5-10 MINS | DIFFICULTY: EASY

500ml cream

125g sugar

10g powdered gelatine or 1 sheet leaf gelatine

½ tsp good quality vanilla extract

½ tsp rosewater

500ml natural yoghurt

6 tamarillos, poached, skins removed

1 cup white chocolate, chopped

Pinch of salt

Heat cream gently in a medium pot, add sugar and stir to dissolve.

Sprinkle the powdered gelatine over a little water and leave to bloom. If using leaf gelatine, soak in water to soften then squeeze to remove excess water.

Remove cream from the heat and mix the gelatine through until fully dissolved.

Stir vanilla and rosewater through the yoghurt then add to the cream mixture.

Pour mixture into 6 moulds (200-250ml capacity) and leave to set in the fridge overnight.

To make the caramelised white chocolate, scatter chopped white chocolate (I use Whittaker's or some other fair trade chocolate) on a baking tray and sprinkle with a pinch of salt. Cook in a moderate oven (180°C) for 5-10 minutes until it starts to brown.

Remove and run a fork through it. Leave it to set. Some will have the consistency of crumbs, which is what you're after.

When ready to serve, carefully run a rubber spatula around the edge of each dessert and upturn onto a plate. Add a poached tamarillo and scatter over caramelised white chocolate crumbs.

Notes: All the components in this recipe can be made in advance.

To poach the tamarillos, simmer them in a little water for about 8 minutes or until tender.

MALVA PUDDING

In 2003, my husband and I moved to beautiful Cape Town, where we lived for a few years. We were introduced to this delicious South African dessert by a family friend. It is such an easy pudding to make and oh so yummy. Be warned though, it is rich and not good for the waistline.

Monique Thomas

SERVES: 6 | PREP: 10 MINS | COOK: 40 MINS | DIFFICULTY: BASIC

60g butter

½ cup caster sugar

½ cup apricot jam

1 Tbsp white vinegar

1 large egg, beaten

½ cup milk

1 cup plain flour

1 tsp baking powder

1 tsp baking soda

SAUCE:

½ cup cold water

100g butter

½ cup caster sugar

1 cup cream

1 tsp vanilla bean paste

Preheat oven to 180°C.

Cream butter and sugar and then whisk in the apricot jam and vinegar.

Whisk the egg and milk, a little at a time, into the above mixture.

Sift together the plain flour, baking powder and baking soda and fold into the wet ingredients.

Grease a 24cm round baking dish, spoon the mixture in and bake for 40 minutes.

To make the sauce, gently heat all ingredients together until the butter has melted.

When the pudding is baked, spoon the sauce over while it's hot.

Notes: It will seem like there's a lot of sauce but it absorbs into the pudding.

Serve with ice cream, custard or cream (or a combination to be really decadent).

Bianca Howlett

MAGAZINE OF DREAMS

For Bianca Howlett, holding the first issue of Junction was a dream come true. 'I've worked in publishing all my life and I've always wanted to start a magazine.'

The popular monthly showcases local creators, makers, food and wine from Puhoi to Waipu, with fascinating back stories of people you'll meet at the market or the school playground.

Junction launched in October 2015, at a time when many questioned the future of publishing. 'Newspapers still play a huge role by informing and connecting society,' says Bianca. 'In an era of content overload, Junction stands for positivity, beauty and creativity.'

Bianca learned the publishing trade through a variety of roles in newspapers, magazines and lifestyle publications in the UK, New Zealand and Western Australia, where she met her husband Clinton.

'Junction champions the community and I hope encourages all of us to support locals'

The pair relocated to Matakana in 2015, drawn by the creative community, natural beauty and for children Lucy and Otis, the availability of a Montessori education in the dedicated class at Matakana Primary School. Not to mention that dream of founding a stylish lifestyle magazine.

In addition to the magazine and the annual Junction Handbook destination guide, Bianca organises the hotly-contested Junction Business Awards, The Oyster and Wine Festival Matakana and monthly 'In Love with Local' networking gatherings. 'Junction champions the community and I hope encourages all of us to support locals,' says Bianca.

While she loves to showcase local cuisine in Junction, at home Bianca favours simple family classics, like this rice pudding. 'My recipe has loads of sugar and naughty stuff, but there's nothing nicer than the aroma of rice pudding baking in the oven on a winter's day.'

RICE PUDDING

My mum taught me how to make no-fuss meals with whatever you had in the cupboard. Rice pudding is one of her favourite dishes.

Bianca Howlett

SERVES: 6-8 | PREP: 15 MINS | COOK: 90-110 MINS | DIFFICULTY: BASIC

4 cups milk

600ml cream

1 cup medium grain rice

1 cup caster sugar

1 Tbsp vanilla essence

1-2 tsp nutmeg

Preheat oven to 180°C.

Combine all ingredients in a large pot. Bring to the boil, remove from the heat and leave to rest for 10 minutes.

Pour the mixture into a 2 litre ovenproof dish. Sprinkle extra nutmeg over the top and bake for 90-110 minutes or until the top is golden brown.

824
830

Emily & Nico Bonnaud

TOUR DU CHOCOLAT

Talking to Nico and Emily Bonnaud, it's tempting to think that the secret to a winning marriage might just lie in chocolate.

Emily is a designer with an eye for artisanship and gorgeous packaging. Nico is a French chocolatier and pastry chef, who honed his palate and his nose in prestigious kitchens around the globe.

After coming 'home' to New Zealand to begin married life, the couple decided it was time to marry their skills as well. And so Honest Chocolat was born. An online store was swiftly followed by a retail shop in Matakana Village, where only a glass window separates customers from the kitchen.

'We wanted customers to see that these chocolates are made here, by hand and with all this care and attention,' says Emily. 'And we can talk to them about chocolate. There's so much to learn, like the fact that cocoa beans are actually white, or that chocolate tastes so different depending where it is grown.'

'These chocolates are made here, by hand, with care and attention'

Yes, just like coffee and wine, soil conditions and farming processes affect the final flavour of the chocolate. Bolivian chocolate has a fruity taste, while chocolate from the Congo is more earthy and smooth.

The couple use only organic, fair trade, 'single origin' chocolate, paired with natural ingredients to bring out the flavour. 'We use the best chocolate that Nico has found and because it is high quality, it tastes lovely from the beginning,' says Emily. 'We don't need to add sugar or cream to make it taste good.'

The couple's passion and commitment to artisanship are evident in the eye-catching presentation and clean, fresh tastes of the award-winning Honest Chocolat. 'We just love the creativity of coming up with new flavours and designs,' says Emily. 'It not only looks beautiful, it tastes amazing too.'

TIRAMISU CHOCOLATE TRUFFLES

This is a more traditional take on our popular tiramisu water ganache bonbon, in the form of a chocolate truffle. This version uses cream and is easy enough to make at home. Perfect as an after dinner treat.

Nico & Emily Bonnaud

SERVES: 60 | PREP: 1 HOUR + CHILLING | COOK: 15 MINUTES | DIFFICULTY: MEDIUM

60g coffee beans

250g liquid cream

4 Tbsp water

40g sugar

300g 70% dark chocolate

40g butter, diced, at room temperature

COATING:

200g 70% dark chocolate

200g cacao powder

Using a mortar and pestle, crush the coffee beans.

In a pan, add cream, water and sugar. Bring to the boil then add the crushed coffee beans and take off the heat. Cover the pan with cling wrap and leave it to infuse for 5 minutes, then strain. In the meantime, chop 300g of dark chocolate and put it in a stainless steel bowl.

Pour half of the strained liquid over the chocolate and slowly mix using a whisk. Pour in the remaining liquid and mix well until all the chocolate is dissolved. Add the diced butter and mix well to form the chocolate ganache.

Pour the ganache into a rectangular tin lined with cling wrap. Once evenly poured, cover the ganache with another layer of cling wrap. Press the cling wrap down to touch the top of the ganache to avoid a skin forming on the top. Place in the freezer for about 2 hours.

To finish, melt 200g of dark chocolate in a bowl over simmering water. Pour the cacao powder into a glass dish. Take the ganache out of the freezer and cut small rectangles (about 1cm by 2.5cm). Once cut, put them back in the freezer to keep cold.

To coat the truffle, simply add a small amount of melted chocolate in your hand. Roll one truffle at a time in it, making sure it is fully covered in a thin layer of chocolate, then drop into the cacao powder. Once all the truffles are coated, take them out of the cacao powder and using a sieve, gently shake off any excess cacao powder.

Notes: Store in an airtight container in the fridge and eat at room temperature to experience the full flavours of the chocolate.

Ascension

KENTISH APPLE TART

This recipe is a favourite of Lucy Smythe from the days when she was a wee nipper at Matakana Primary.

From the Kitchen of Dyson Smythe & Gladwell Lawyers

SERVES: 6 | PREP: 30 MINS | COOK: 40 MINS | DIFFICULTY: EASY

PASTRY CRUST:

1 cup flour

½ cup sugar

Pinch of salt

100g butter

FILLING:

Grated rind of 1 lemon

1 Tbsp lemon juice

⅓ cup sugar

25g melted butter

3 medium apples (tart ones are better)

1 egg, beaten

Preheat oven to 190°C.

To make the pastry crust, place all ingredients in a food processor and mix until it resembles breadcrumbs.

Press into a greased pie or flan dish.

To make the filling, mix lemon rind, juice, sugar and butter.

Peel and grate the apples and add to the filling mixture.

Add the beaten egg, pour into the crust and smooth the top.

Bake for 35-40 minutes.

Ascension
WINE ESTATE

TIRAMISU

The perfect classic Italian dessert with a twist.

From the Kitchen of Ascension Wine Estate

SERVES: 4 | PREP: 20 MINS + CHILLING | COOK: 10 MINS | DIFFICULTY: EASY

6 egg yolks

1 cup sugar

330ml double cream

225g mascarpone

1 shot espresso

50ml Ascension 'Fortitude' Tawny Port

50ml Marsala dessert wine

50ml cream

10ml vanilla essence

175g sponge lady finger biscuits

25g chunk dark chocolate, grated

Cocoa powder

Combine egg yolks and sugar in the top of a double boiler, over boiling water. Reduce the heat to low and cook for about 10-12 minutes, stirring until the egg yolks become thick and lemon-coloured.

Remove from heat and allow to cool then whip gently.

In a separate bowl, mix the cream until it becomes firm.

Add mascarpone cheese to the cool yolks and beat until combined.

Gently fold the whipped cream into the mascarpone mixture.

For the liquid preparation, mix espresso with port, Marsala, cream and vanilla essence.

Dip the lady fingers for 3-4 seconds until they are nicely soaked, but not soggy.

Layer the biscuits into your glasses then spread the creamy mixture on top. Repeat the layers 2 times and finish with grated chocolate.

Cover and chill for a few hours or overnight.

To serve, dust with cocoa powder and grate over the remainder of the chocolate.

Notes: Tiramisu can be kept in the fridge for up to 2 days.

Beautifully situated amongst the vines of Matakana, Ascension Wine Estate is the perfect location for wine tasting, lunch and dinner.
Ascension can also host stunning weddings and stylish corporate events in the Belfry, a fully self-contained function centre, as well as many locations stretched over the estate.
Ascension Wine Estate Ltd.
480 Matakana Rd
Matakana
Warkworth, 0985
09 422 9601
021 885 554
functions@ascensionwine.co.nz
Ascension
WINE ESTATE

The PTA Bake Sale at Matakana School is the most anticipated morning tea on the village calendar. Happy kids skip across the playground, gold coin in hand, to join the jiggling queue of hungry little shoppers craning their necks to choose their treats.

Oh what to eat? A gorgeous cupcake? Good old-fashioned caramel slice? Chocolate brownie? Or a piece of whatever Mum sent in that morning (because Mum's baking is always the best).

Our baking chapter acknowledges the love that goes into filling those tins and honours the everyday contributions of Matakana parents to raise funds for our school.

We hope you enjoy replenishing your tins with these favourite baking recipes, and new twists on lunchbox classics.

Baking

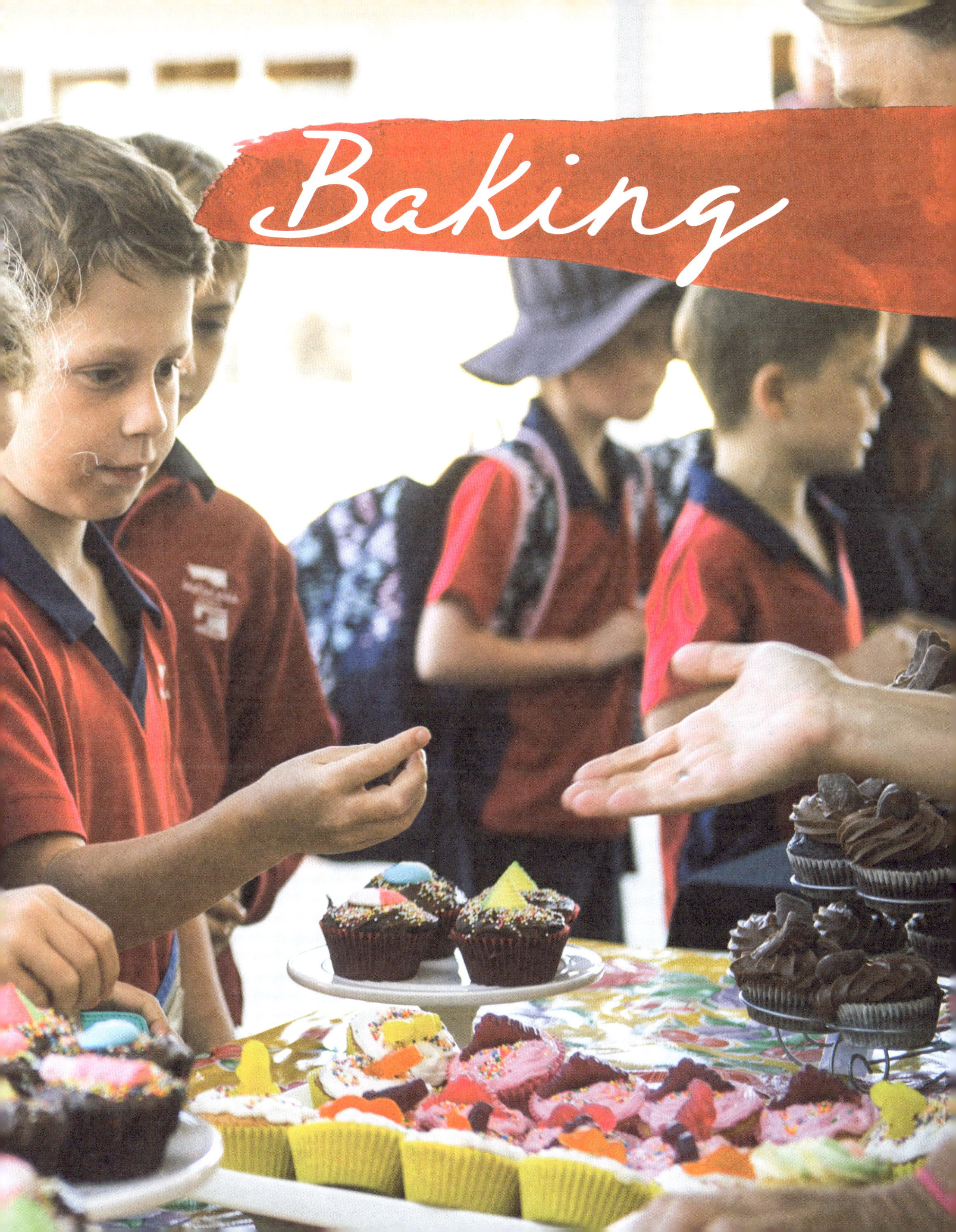

MATAKANA
SCHOOL

MATAKANA
SCHOOL

MATAKAN
SCHOOL

BLUEBERRY CAKE

My mother was at a dinner party in the 1980s where they served this cake. She loved it so much she asked for the recipe, which came from a friend of hers who was a chef. She has used the recipe for years and people are always so impressed with it!

Kat Carter

SERVES: 6 | PREP: 20 MINS | COOK: 1 HOUR | DIFFICULTY: BASIC

BASE:

1 cup flour

½ cup sugar

1½ tsp baking powder

1 egg

1 tsp vanilla essence

½ cup butter, softened

3 cups blueberries

TOPPING:

2½ cups blueberries

2 cups sour cream

2 egg yolks

½ cup sugar

1 tsp vanilla essence

Preheat oven to 180°C.

Combine base ingredients, mix thoroughly and spread into a greased 25cm springform cake tin.

Sprinkle the blueberries evenly over the mixture.

Combine topping ingredients and mix well. Pour over the base and blueberries.

Bake for 1 hour or until custard topping is firm and lightly browned.

Also great served with ice cream as a dessert.

Heiko Besgens

THIS DAILY BREAD

In the mid-1980s, Heiko Besgens said 'auf Wiedersehen' to Germany, in search of a freer life. He tried Canada... too cold. He tried Fiji... too hot. He found Aotearoa... just right.

'I love how everyone is deeply integrated,' he says, his eyes alight. 'I love how a coffee culture has developed, I love that Kiwis are curious. Most countries are driven by big industry. Here there's still room for niches.'

The Berlin-born baker learned his craft in Cologne, undertaking a three-year apprenticeship followed by two years at the Master Bakers Academy. 'Bread has been a staple of mankind for thousands of years,' he says.

'Sourdough loaves are my favourite. The crust caramelises from the natural sugars in the grains, it's easier to digest and it's healthier'

When Plume Café opened its doors in 2012, Heiko took over the bakery and began his daily ritual of rising at 3am to knead, sculpt and fashion delicious breads, brioches and baked goodies. 'At Plume Café I can bake to my heart's content.'

'Sourdough loaves are my favourite. The crust caramelises from the natural sugars in the grains, it's easier to digest and it's healthier,' says Heiko. 'But sourdough culture is high maintenance. I look after mine like a baby.'

Word of Heiko's delicious breads soon spread and assistant baker Monish Naicker joined the bakery team in 2016. The pair are renowned for their hot cross buns and the elaborate gingerbread house they create for local children to enjoy at Christmas.

Heiko's buttery brioche is a favourite in the café, best enjoyed with lashings of butter and a great cup of coffee.

HEIKO'S BUTTERY BRIOCHE

This simple to make version of the traditional French brioche is golden on the outside, soft on the inside and is a real crowd pleaser.

Heiko Bergers

SERVES: 6 | PREP: 20 MINS + CHILL OVERNIGHT + PROVING | COOK: 15-18 MINS | DIFFICULTY: EASY

- **500g flour**
- **50g sugar**
- **10g salt**
- **250g butter, at room temperature**
- **4 eggs (size 6)**
- **85ml milk**
- **25g fresh yeast (or 20g dry yeast)**

Mix all ingredients together in a food processor for 5-7 minutes (or 10-12 minutes if mixing by hand) until well combined and smooth. The mixture will be sticky.

Place the dough in a lightly oiled metal or plastic bowl, cover with a cloth and place in the fridge overnight. This allows the flavours to infuse.

The next morning, remove the dough from the fridge and allow to sit (covered to retain moistness) for an hour at room temperature. Prove until the dough has almost doubled.

Preheat oven to 190°C. Cut the dough into six even portions then roll them into a soft ball and pop each in a greased muffin tin.

Bake for 15-18 minutes or until golden brown.

Pull pieces off, slather on some butter and enjoy with some great New Zealand coffee.

APPLE SPICE CAKE

This moist cake keeps and travels well. Invariably it comes out slightly different each time - a tribute to nature and the difference between one apple and another.

The Gibson Family

SERVES: 8 | PREP: 20 MINS | COOK: 45 MINS | DIFFICULTY: EASY

125g butter

1 cup cooked apples (about 2-3 apples) or 1 x 225g can apples

1 cup sugar

1 egg

1¼ cups flour

1 tsp cinnamon

½ tsp nutmeg

½ tsp allspice

½ tsp salt

1 tsp baking soda

½ cup sultanas

Icing sugar

Preheat oven to 150°C.

Grease a 20cm cake tin.

Melt butter in a medium - large pot.

Remove from heat and add the apples and sugar. Stir to combine then add the egg and mix.

Sift the dry ingredients and add this to the apple mixture together with the sultanas.

Combine just enough to blend ingredients evenly.

Spread the mixture into the prepared tin and bake for 45 minutes.

Allow to cool and then sprinkle with icing sugar.

Notes: To make as muffins, grease a 12 capacity muffin tray and divide the mixture evenly (allow ½ cup per muffin).

Bake until risen and set (about 35 minutes).

Stand for 5 minutes before turning out.

Mark & Tia Wooller

THE ART OF GREEN LIVING

Fingers are always green at Mark and Tia Wooller's house. Some are green with oil paint from renowned artist Mark's landscape-inspired paintings. Others are green from tending the gardens, blending green smoothies, or leading tiny students from Tia's onsite Montessori preschool on expeditions through bush and meadow.

For two decades, the couple have lived out their passions on these three acres. When they bought the land it was bare, with an old farmhouse, but a boundary of mature totara and close proximity to a lovely village school sealed the deal.

'I used to pinch myself driving up the valley – I couldn't believe we lived here'

'I used to pinch myself driving up the valley – I couldn't believe we lived here,' says Tia. 'There were lots of like-minded people, a really friendly community, growing their own food or into organics'.

Together, they built a life that enabled their passions to flourish. 'We co-parented our three children around our work,' says Mark.

First, they planted an heirloom orchard, and hundreds of other native and ornamental trees for seasonal bursts of colour. They created walking trails, installed sculptures, chooks and beehives, and cultivated an extensive veggie garden to sustain the family's mostly-vegetarian lifestyle.

Then they built the preschool, a continuation of Tia's passion for education. She has since taught over a thousand Matakana children and one group of parents were so inspired, they established a Montessori primary class at Matakana School.

Finally, Mark set up his studio. 'The garden, the flowers and foliage are all the inspiration I need.'

UPSIDE DOWN PLUM CAKE

Our Marabella plum was the first tree in our heritage orchard to produce great quantities of fruit. We make this cake every year to herald the start of summer.

Tia & Mark Wooller

SERVES: 6-8 | PREP: 40 MINS | COOK: 45 MINS | DIFFICULTY: BASIC

125g sugar

70ml water

300g plums, halved, stone removed

150g butter, at room temperature

150g sugar

4 eggs

5 Tbsp ground almonds

200g self raising flour

Preheat oven to 180°C. Line a round cake tin with baking paper.

Combine sugar and water in a pot and stir over a medium heat until the sugar is dissolved. Then cook without stirring until the sugar caramelises and remove from the heat. This takes about 20 minutes.

Cream the butter and sugar, add eggs one at a time, stirring to combine. Beat in the ground almonds and a few tablespoons of flour. Gently fold in the remaining flour until mixed. It will have a thick consistency.

Pour the hot syrup into the tin, immediately arrange the plums, cut side down, over the base. This will be the top of the cake when it is finished.

Spoon the batter mixture over the plums. Bake for 40-45 minutes until firm in the middle and the edges are slightly shrunk back from the sides of the pan.

Leave to cool then place a large plate over the top of the tin and quickly invert - beware of hot syrup!

Serve warm with cream, yoghurt or a good vanilla ice cream.

Fun & games at school camp

Camp Bentzon, Kawau Island

Angela Corinaldi

ICING ON THE COMMUNITY CAKE

Many parents will be familiar with the night before birthday party scramble, when the cake collapses in the tin, there is a giant tear in the fondant icing, and the end result looks nothing like the picture in the book.

That's unless you know Angela Corinaldi.

This former contender for the world artistic roller skating championship (think Torvill and Dean on wheels) has a gift for turning out Pinterest-perfect cakes.

She started playing with buttercream icing on her son Luca's second birthday and was soon experimenting with more elaborate creations for family and friends. Before long her delectable treats were in hot demand for local events and parties.

From R2D2 to unicorns and rainbows, every creation is different. 'One brief was for a crocodile swamp with snakes on rocks,' she laughs. 'Another was a replica of a beloved hot rod. The most challenging cake, based on a red 1966 El Camino car, took 30 hours.'

> ***'I love seeing the joy on the kids' faces when they find "their" piece of cake'***

Luca had barely started at Matakana School when Angela raised her hand for the PTA, which she chaired from 2013 to 2016. 'I love engaging with the community.'

Along with the fundraising and organising, there was baking. Her gorgeous cupcakes fly off the stand at PTA bake sales and Angela's graduation cakes, emblazoned with every child's name, have been a treasured school tradition since 2013.

'I love seeing the joy on the kids' faces when they find "their" piece of cake', says Angela. 'That's what makes it so special.'

GRADUATION CHOCOLATE CAKE

I've made this cake for every school graduation since 2013 and countless parents have asked for the recipe. I hope that when they bake the cake, they remember their child's graduation from Matakana School.

Angela Corinaldi

SERVES: 10 | PREP: 20 MINS | COOK: 40-55 MINS | DIFFICULTY: EASY

125g butter, softened

⅔ cup sugar

½ cup icing sugar

1¼ cups self raising flour (or plain flour and 2 tsp baking powder)

1 tsp baking soda

Pinch of salt

½ cup cocoa powder

2 eggs

1 cup milk

1 tsp vanilla extract

Preheat oven to 180°C. Lightly grease and flour a 20-23cm cake tin or use baking paper if preferred.

Cream butter, sugar and icing sugar in a food processor.

Sift the flour, baking soda and salt into a mixing bowl with the butter and sugar mixture.

Add all remaining ingredients and mix until all the ingredients are just combined. Do not overmix.

Pour into prepared tin and bake for 35-50 minutes. Ice with buttercream or chocolate ganache.

Notes: Do not open the oven during baking. To avoid an overcooked dry cake, test with a skewer or knife after 35 minutes. If it comes out clean the cake is cooked. If not, cook for longer and keep testing at 5 minute intervals until you get a clean skewer/knife.

Year 6 Graduation picnic and beach swim

GLUTEN FREE CHOCOLATE BROWNIE

Our family loves chocolate brownies and this gluten free recipe from my sister-in-law Sonja, is more delicious than our non gluten-free version.

Sandra Bolland

SERVES: 8 | PREP: 15 MINS | COOK: 45 MINS | DIFFICULTY: BASIC

2 cups caster sugar

¾ cup cocoa powder

½ cup rice flour

1 tsp baking powder

4 eggs, beaten

250g unsalted butter, melted

2 tsp vanilla extract

200g dark chocolate, chopped

Preheat oven to 160°C.

Line a 22cm square tin with baking paper.

Place all but last 2 ingredients in a mixing bowl and mix on low speed for 30 seconds, before mixing for a further minute on medium to high speed.

Spoon mixture into the prepared tin and bake for 40-45 minutes or until just set.

Remove from the oven and allow to cool completely before slicing into squares.

Dust with icing sugar and serve with whipped cream.

IRISH TEA BREAD

As an avid runner, an elderly gentleman introduced me to off-road marathon running across English bridleways and footpaths, where refreshments were provided along the route and at the end. This is how I discovered this wonderful Irish Tea Bread, which is now a family favourite. This recipe was originally printed in a 1950s church magazine of St Mary at Stoke.

The Christy Family

SERVES: 20 | PREP: 20 MINS + SOAKING | COOK: 1½ HOURS | DIFFICULTY: BASIC

400ml boiling water

2 English Breakfast tea bags

500g mixed dried fruit

200g brown sugar

1 egg

½ tsp mixed spice

250g self raising flour

Preheat oven to 175°C.

Brew tea. Put dried fruit in the mixing bowl and add the tea (minus teabags). Leave to soak for at least 2 hours but preferably longer i.e. overnight.

Mix sugar, egg and spice. Mix in the flour.

Line a loaf tin with baking paper. Pour mixture into the tin.

Bake for about 1½ hours until the skewer comes out clean from the centre but do not overcook.

Serve warm or cold, spread with butter.

LEMON SHORTBREAD

There are two Nanas in our family and to differentiate them the boys started calling one Nana Bickie, as she always brings baking when she visits. This is one of Nana Bickie's recipes.

The Garthwaite Family

SERVES: 20 | PREP: 10 MINS + CHILLING | COOK: 20 MINS | DIFFICULTY: EASY

225g butter
1 cup icing sugar
½ tsp vanilla essence
1⅔ cup flour
1 cup cornflour
Rind of 1 lemon

Preheat oven to 150°C.

Cream butter and icing sugar until white and fluffy. Add vanilla essence.

Gradually work in the flour, cornflour and lemon rind until combined.

Divide the mixture and make two rolls (sausages).

Wrap in grease proof paper and chill in the fridge for 20 minutes.

Slice the rolls into 1cm biscuits and use a fork to prick two rows of holes.

Bake for 20 minutes.

Matakana
COUNTRY
PARK

LEMON PISTACHIO CAKE

This is a lovely afternoon tea or dessert cake. The recipe was given to me by a dear friend in the UK who cooks rather well. Perfect served hot with yoghurt on the side.

Pam Boss

SERVES: 10 | PREP: 20 MINS | COOK: 50-55 MINS | DIFFICULTY: BASIC

- **60g unsalted pistachios, shelled**
- **60g ground almonds**
- **60g breadcrumbs**
- **200g caster sugar**
- **2½ tsp baking powder**
- **Zest of 1 lemon**
- **200ml olive oil**
- **4 eggs**
- **Juice of 1 lemon**
- **30g coconut sugar (or other sugar)**
- **Extra pistachios, roughly chopped**
- **Lemon zest, extra**

Grease a 20-23cm cake tin and line the base only with baking paper.

Process the pistachios into a powder or very finely chop. Mix with ground almonds, breadcrumbs, caster sugar, baking powder and lemon zest.

Mix the oil and the eggs and beat lightly. Stir these into the dry ingredients.

Pour into the greased tin and place in a cold oven.

Turn the oven on to 180°C and bake for 50-55 minutes.

If the top starts to go too brown put a piece of baking paper lightly over the top of the tin whilst baking. It will be ready when it looks like it is coming away from the side of the tin.

To make the syrup, put lemon juice and coconut sugar into a small pot and bring to the boil. Reduce heat to a simmer for 5-10 minutes.

Remove cake from the tin, turn it over and put it onto a plate bottom side up. Remove paper carefully. Pierce it all over with a skewer and drizzle the syrup over the cake.

Just before serving, add chopped pistachios and scatter lemon zest on top for decoration.

Notes: You can make the breadcrumbs out of bread with seeds or gluten-free bread if preferred.

MALAYSIAN COCONUT SLICE

My Mum brought me back a cookbook from a restaurant she enjoyed in Rarotonga - and everything in it is delicious, especially this slice! This recipe is by Sue Carruthers.

The Ashwell Family

SERVES: 25 SLICES (APPROX) | PREP: 10-15 MINS | COOK: 50 MINS | DIFFICULTY: EASY

4 eggs

1½ cups white sugar

⅔ cup flour

½ tsp baking powder

120g butter, melted, cooled

2 cups desiccated coconut, divided

1 tsp vanilla essence

¼ cup brown sugar

Preheat oven to 180°C.

Grease a 20cm square cake tin (preferably with a removable base) and line with baking paper.

Beat the eggs lightly. Add the white sugar ½ cup at a time and beat until well combined.

Sift flour and baking powder together and fold into the egg mixture with the butter, 1½ cups of coconut and vanilla. Spread into the tin.

Mix the remaining ½ cup of coconut and the brown sugar together and sprinkle on top of the cake.

Bake for 50 minutes until firm to touch and it is leaving the sides of the cake tin.

Cover with foil after 20 minutes to prevent cake getting too brown.

Notes: Absolutely delicious and so easy, especially as it uses basic, everyday pantry ingredients.

SPELT CHOC CHIP COOKIES

A little treat for the lunch box.

Gabrielle, Andre & Ziggy

SERVES: 20 | PREP: 10 MINS | COOK: 10 MINS | DIFFICULTY: EASY

125g butter

¼ cup sugar

1 tsp vanilla

2 eggs

2 cups spelt flour

1 cup desiccated coconut

1 tsp baking powder

½ cup choc chips

Preheat oven to 180°C.

Cream butter and sugar. Add vanilla and eggs (one at a time), mixing well.

In another bowl combine spelt flour, coconut and baking powder. Fold dry ingredients into creamed butter and mix well.

Fold choc chips into the biscuit batter.

Spoon small amounts and flatten with a fork onto a greased tray.

Bake for 8-10 minutes.

CARROT CAKE

This cake never fails and everyone comments that it's the best carrot cake they have ever tasted.

Clair McEntegart

SERVES: 15 | PREP: 15 MINS | COOK: 45 MINS | DIFFICULTY: BASIC

3 eggs
¾ cup oil
2 cups raw sugar
3 cups carrot, grated
2 cups wholemeal flour
2 tsp baking powder
2 tsp baking soda
1 tsp cinnamon
1 tsp mixed spice
1 tsp nutmeg
¾ cup fruit juice

Preheat oven to 170°C.

Grease a 20cm cake tin and line with baking paper.

Mix eggs, oil and sugar until light and fluffy. Grate the carrots and add to the egg mix.

In a separate bowl, place all the dry ingredients and fold into the carrot/egg mix.

Add juice slowly until the mixture is wet but not too runny.

Place into the baking tin and bake for approximately 45 minutes.

When cool, ice with cream cheese icing.

Spinning
Wheel

GALA CREW

COFFEE

Authentic
ORIGINAL

GALA CREW

All the fun of the fair at the Matakana School Gala

PEANUT BUTTER CARAMEL SLICE

The caramel in this slice is made from peanut butter! It is really easy, won't fail and is a real crowd pleaser. Warning, this recipe is not healthy and should be shared at large gatherings.

The Hooper Family

SERVES: 30 | PREP: 20 MINS + CHILLING | NO COOKING | DIFFICULTY: EASY

BASE:

250g chocolate digestive biscuits, crushed

395g can sweetened condensed milk

1 Tbsp cocoa

½ cup desiccated coconut

FILLING:

250g smooth peanut butter

80g butter, at room temperature

Pinch of salt

1½ cups icing sugar

CHOCOLATE ICING:

200g milk chocolate

1 Tbsp vegetable oil

Grease and line a 20cm square (or 20cm x 30cm rectangle) slice tin with baking paper.

Combine the base ingredients in a large bowl. Press the mixture firmly into the prepared tin and refrigerate.

Combine the peanut butter, butter and salt in a food processor and process on medium speed until the mixture is smooth.

Sift in the icing sugar and process again until smooth and thick.

Spread the mixture over the base and smooth it out. Refrigerate while you make the chocolate icing.

Melt the chocolate in a heat proof bowl over a pot of simmering water. Add the oil and stir until smooth. Allow to cool slightly and then pour evenly over the slice. Refrigerate for at least two hours.

Slice and serve.

Notes: You can also use dark chocolate for the icing.

Keep in an airtight container in the fridge.

RHUBARB & RASPBERRY SHORTCAKE

This recipe came from our grandmother, Jill Keith. She used to make it many years ago in her café, the Longwood Palm Garden Café in Point Wells.

Olivia & Emily Maginley

SERVES: 18 | PREP: 15 MINS | COOK: 40-60 MINS | DIFFICULTY: BASIC

250g butter
1½ cups sugar
2 eggs
3 cups flour
2 tsp baking powder

FRUIT FILLING:
5 cups rhubarb, chopped
2 cups frozen raspberries
4 Tbsp cornflour
¾ cup sugar

TOPPING:
Cinnamon sugar
Flaked almonds

Preheat oven to 180°C.

Line a 25cm x 30cm tin with baking paper.

To make the crust, cream butter and sugar, add eggs and beat well.

Mix the flour and baking powder together and add to the egg mixture (add extra flour if it is too sticky to handle).

Press half the crust mixture into the tin.

For the fruit filling, mix all ingredients together and place on top of the crust. Crumble the remaining dough roughly on top, leaving some fruit exposed.

Sprinkle with cinnamon sugar and flaked almonds.

Bake for 45 minutes to 1 hour (time varies and different fruits take longer to cook).

Notes: If you don't have raspberries, you can substitute with apples and feijoas.

Matakana
COUNTRY
PARK

FEIJOA BANANA CAKE

This is a great, moist cake that is easy enough for our girls to whip up by themselves. If you don't have feijoas, leave them out and make it a banana cake.

Janine King

SERVES: 12 | PREP: 10 MINS | COOK: 45 MINS | DIFFICULTY: EASY

5 feijoas

2½ cups mashed banana

2½ cups self raising flour

1 tsp baking soda

1 cup oil

1 cup sugar

4 eggs

1 tsp vanilla essence

Preheat oven to 160°C.

Blend feijoas (skin on) and bananas together in a food processor.

Place all ingredients into a bowl and combine until smooth.

Grease a 23cm springform tin and pour ingredients in.

Bake in the oven for 45 minutes.

Top with either cream cheese icing or icing with grated lemon zest.

Notes: Keep over-ripe bananas and feijoas in the freezer.

Leaving the skin on the feijoas gives a texture to the cake, however, they can be removed if you prefer.

Matakana
COUNTRY
PARK

SWEDISH GINGER BISCUITS

(BIRGITTAS PEPPARKAKOR)

This is a recipe handed down from my Swedish Grandmother, Gunvar Maule. My mum used to bake them only at Christmas, so they have a special place amongst our family Christmas traditions. My mum would even bake larger versions to use as place settings, with everyone's names iced onto them.

The Cullen Family

SERVES: 75-100 BISCUITS | PREP: 10 MINS | COOK: 8 MINS | DIFFICULTY: BASIC

- **225g brown sugar**
- **225g margarine**
- **1 egg**
- **1 Tbsp golden syrup or honey**
- **425g plain flour**
- **2 tsp baking soda**
- **2 tsp ground ginger**
- **2 tsp ground cinnamon**
- **¼ tsp ground cloves**

This recipe is made over two days.

DAY 1:

Cream the margarine and sugar together, then beat in the egg gradually and the syrup or honey.

Mix the flour and baking soda together. Add some flour to the egg mixture if it seems to curdle and mix in the spices to form a dough. Work with the hands. If it is too sticky to do this then add a little more flour until it leaves the hands and the bowl "clean".

Divide the dough into 4 equal parts and form into balls. Place into a bowl, covering it with foil or cling wrap and refrigerate overnight.

DAY 2:

Preheat oven to 200°C.

Grease and flour a baking tray.

Flour your work-top and roll out one ball of dough as thin as possible. Cut out shapes and carefully slide a spatula under the biscuits and place them on the baking tray.

Bake for approximately 8 minutes. Be aware that they burn very easily!

Matakana
COUNTRY
PARK

STICKY DATE LOAF

One of John Baker's favourite and easy recipes which he enjoys eating with friends and family.

From the Kitchen of Matakana Country Park

SERVES: 10 | PREP: 20 MINS | COOK: 30-40 MINS

1¼ cups dates

1¼ cups boiling water

1 tsp baking soda

60g butter

¾ cup brown sugar

2 eggs

1 cup flour

12 dates (extra), finely chopped

Preheat oven to 180°C.

Combine dates and boiling water in a large pot and bring to the boil then immediately remove from the heat.

Stir in baking soda and allow to stand for 5 minutes.

Blend the date mixture with butter and sugar. Add eggs, flour and extra chopped dates until just combined.

Bake in a lined loaf tin for 30-40 minutes.

Heineken

Bramble
Espresso Shop & Honest Canteen

The Matakana Country Park is set within a gorgeous 50-acre country estate, located just one hour north of Auckland and just over the hill from the Matakana Village - surrounded by thousands of acres of protected regional parks, marine reserves, boutique vineyards, lush valleys and beautiful beaches. The perfect setting for weddings and events and if you are lucky - catch one of the fabulous concerts often held over the summer season.

On a daily basis - The Park hosts a wide range of family-friendly activities (not to mention plenty of parking). From the animal experience, miniature ride-on train, horse and carriage rides, bicycle hire and adventure playground to a spot of shopping at the Craft Co-op for souvenirs and the Art Gallery.

Start your day with breakfast at Bramble Café and finish with dinner at the famous Stables Restaurant, or enjoy a light bite to eat and a drink at Smith's Bar. Fun for all the family!!

Matakana Country Park

1151 Leigh Road, Matakana

usually open 7 days

www.matakanacountrypark.co.nz

info@matakanacountrypark.co.nz

www.facebook.com/matakanacountrypark

Matakana COUNTRY PARK

JOY TO THE PEOPLE

Totem Retreat

Stay. Experience. Nurture the Soul.

To book boutique group or family accommodation or for information on upcoming workshops and retreats at Totem contact:

021 885 984
totem.retreat@gmail.com
www.totemretreat.co.nz

Resource Planning Inc.

Explore your property's potential.

We are your trusted local experts for quality environmental planning and resource consent advice, including visitor accommodation, subdivisions and minor dwellings. We manage the whole process, and have a proven track record of timely, accurate, cost-effective and hassle-free consents.

021 618 741
katherine@resourceplanninginc.com
www.resourceplanninginc.com

Christine Sheehy

Copywriter, author, speaker

Brand storytelling, messaging and copywriting for websites, social media, email marketing and press.

Refine your message, engage your tribe, grow your business.

Let's go write to the heart of your business

021 0200 9595
christine@christinesheehy.co
www.christinesheehy.co

Redgraves Home Fabrics

'Harakeke' by Louis Alexander Textiles, exclusively available at Redgraves Home Fabrics.

Quality curtains, blinds, shutters and upholstery, custom-made for your home or beach house.

Free in-home design consultation Auckland-wide, including Matakana, Omaha & Warkworth.

09 476 9102
www.redgraveshomefabrics.co.nz

Black and White Barn

Luxury studio accommodation in an architecturally designed property. Black and White Barn is a two minute walk to the vibrant Matakana Village and Markets, a central base to explore the surrounding coast - or a sanctuary to dream, sleep and think.

Your host - Amy Hope

0211 211 602
www.blackandwhitebarn.co.nz

Katherine Norman

Landscape and documentary photography, contemporary watercolours and custom artworks inspired by rural Matakana landscapes.

As seen in Homestyle, Your Home & Garden, NZ House & Garden and Junction. Visit the online gallery for original works, prints and Katherine's latest work.

021 618 741
www.katherinenorman.co.nz
@katherine_norman_studio

Coops Design - Auto Wrap NZ

Glenn is a NZ award winning local signwriter who designs, prints and applies signage to almost anything.

Glenn Cooper

0274 917 719
coopsdesignnz@gmail.com

Check us out on
facebook /auto wrap nz

Hamish Macfarlane Builders

Registered Master Builders for quality builds and reliable, honest service.

0275 753 475
hamish.macfarlane@xtra.co.nz
www.hamishmacfarlanebuilders.co.nz

Wharf Street Bistro

6 Wharf Street, Warkworth
09 422 2511

info@wharfstreetbistro.com
www.wharfstreetbistro.com

Omaha Holiday Houses

Fancy a free holiday?

To find out how much your property can earn you while you're on holiday, contact Nicola Hooper of Omaha Holiday Houses on **027 333 3903** for a free appraisal.

Frolic Ceramics

frolicceramics.co.nz
Text **021 575 780**
@frolicceramics

Sugarloaf Lodge

"A haven of quiet sophistication" .... a B&B Retreat, close to Matakana Village with remarkable views over Omaha Bay and out to the Barrier Islands. Total peace and quiet romance. Private Suites in a separate Guest Cottage.

1068 Leigh Rd, Matakana
021 022 69331
www.sugarloaflodge.co.nz

Green with Envy

Home + lifestyle store

Cnr Sharp & Matakana Roads

09 422 7554

www.greenwithenvy.co.nz

Matakana Coastal Walks

Fully catered coastal walks.
Blissful views, great walks, cosy accommodation and excellent food

021 146 0257

www.matakanacoastalwalks.co.nz

Charles Swanston Insurance

Contact Charles for all your health insurance needs. Are you paying too much each month for your insurance? Most of us are! Charles will provide you with a free quote to ensure you are getting the best deal.

021 585 545

Honest Chocolat

Award-winning beautiful chocolates handcrafted in Matakana, using organic, ethically sourced, single-origin chocolate.

Nico and Emily Bonnaud, Shop 1, Matakana Village, 2 Matakana Valley Road, Matakana 0985

09 600 2442 | hello@honestchocolat.com | www.honestchocolat.com

Summer Sessions

Matakana's favourite surf shop, selling surf fashion, wetsuits, wax, surfboards, SUPs and more from brands like Roxy, Rip Curl, Quicksilver, Vissla, Volcom, Seafolly, Rhythm, Silent Theory, RPM, iLabb and others.

44 Matakana Valley Rd, Matakana

09 283 3598 | www.summersessions.co.nz.

BREAKFAST

PICNICS

CANAPÉS

LIGHT MEALS

MAIN MEALS

KAIMOANA

HUNT & GATHER

DESSERTS

BAKING

THANK YOU

It takes a village to create a cookbook...And this book would not have been possible without the hundreds of people who gave so generously of their time, resources and financial support.

We were overwhelmed by the community's response to our request for recipes, and while we couldn't include them all, we were extremely grateful to everyone who took the time to submit their favourite recipes.

We thank our sponsors, your commitment and support from the very beginning enabled us to take our idea forward and give it life.

We thank everyone who has purchased a book and in doing so, supported our school.

To the Whangateau Folk Club, The Vivian Gallery, the Point Wells Connoisseurs Club, Omaha Surf Life Saving Club, the Ti Point kaimoana crew, the Matakana School PTA and the Matakana Green Swap. We thank you for welcoming us to your gatherings and being the stars of our chapter openers.

To Green with Envy, Mooi Mooi, Frolic Ceramics, Quail Farm Collectables and Old School Inc, thanks for providing the wonderful platters, dishes and accessories for our photo shoots.

Thanks also to the Matakana School Board of Trustees for your ongoing encouragement and support, and to Kent Bowyer-Sidwell at Benefitz, whose guidance and advice around the printing has been invaluable.

A huge thanks to our dedicated cookbook team who over the past two years, have given hundreds of hours of professional expertise and personal time to bring this vision to life.

Finally, to our friends in the wider community, thanks for helping to make Matakana a place that is special to us all. We hope you enjoy the product of our collective labour for many years to come.

From the Cookbook Team

Peter Young, Lori Satterthwaite, Christine Sheehy, Kate Arbuthnot, Monique Thomas, Emily Parker, Laurette Macky, Amanda Garthwaite, Sally Jack, Anneliese Parker, Katherine Norman

49
48
88
87